The Kinderchat Guide to Elementary School Projects

The Kinderchat Guide to Elementary School Projects takes the structure, philosophy, and child-centered, playful approach to learning most commonly seen in early childhood and shares how to scale and apply it for the wider elementary school community. From one of the founders of the popular online Kinderchat group, this book shows how inviting play into academic learning forms an essential "back and forth" between application and skill development. Learn how to foster discovery, playfulness, imagination, and spontaneity into the elementary school academic curriculum, while keeping skills in the foreground. Offering lesson plans, scaffolded implementation techniques, and methodologies, these unique and approachable projects are ready to use by in-service elementary educators, seasoned professionals, and school leaders.

Heidi Echternacht is co-founder of Kinderchat, a weekly professional conversation, resource library, and online network for early childhood advocates and educators. Created and led by teachers, Kinderchat has hosted global discussions between and among professional educators and in-service teachers for over ten years. Author of *The Kinderchat Guide to the Classroom*, Heidi has been an educator of children for over 20 years and currently teaches second grade in Princeton, NJ, USA.

The Kinderchat Guide to Elementary School Projects

A Playful Approach to Learning

Heidi Echternacht

NEW YORK AND LONDON

Designed cover image: © Getty Images

First published 2024
by Routledge
605 Third Avenue, New York, NY 10158

and by Routledge
4 Park Square, Milton Park, Abingdon, Oxon, OX14 4RN

Routledge is an imprint of the Taylor & Francis Group, an informa business

© 2024 Heidi Echternacht

The right of Heidi Echternacht to be identified as author of this work has been asserted in accordance with sections 77 and 78 of the Copyright, Designs and Patents Act 1988.

All rights reserved. No part of this book may be reprinted or reproduced or utilised in any form or by any electronic, mechanical, or other means, now known or hereafter invented, including photocopying and recording, or in any information storage or retrieval system, without permission in writing from the publishers.

Trademark notice: Product or corporate names may be trademarks or registered trademarks, and are used only for identification and explanation without intent to infringe.

ISBN: 978-1-032-33422-6 (hbk)
ISBN: 978-1-032-32895-9 (pbk)
ISBN: 978-1-003-31962-7 (ebk)

DOI: 10.4324/9781003319627

Typeset in Palatino
by SPi Technologies India Pvt Ltd (Straive)

For my dad, who taught me to love to learn
my mom, who nurtured my imagination
and to my school community
who allow me to use both.

Contents

Acknowledgements ix

Introduction and Getting Started 1
About Kinderchat 1
The Goals of This Book 3
How to Use This Book 4

1 Projects Philosophy, Definitions, and Structures 6
General Philosophies and Definitions 6
The Skill of Sensemaking 10
Methods and Approaches Surrounding Project Work
and Inquiry 14
How to PBL 23
The Play Projects 25

2 The Town and Neighborhood 47
Towns and Neighborhoods: Philosophy and
Application 47
The Bank 49
The Grocery Store 58
Museums, Kitchens, and Cafes 68
Stoplight Story Theater 74
Toy Town Makerspace 79
Money Town 83

3 Civics and Society 93
Philosophy and Application 93
Math and Social Studies Projects 94
Tic Tac Toe Tournament 94
RISK and Gamer Teams 98
Math Court 102

Math Debate Teams 106
Expanding Circles: Places 112
Literacy and Social Studies Projects 116
Expanding Circles: People 116
The Neighborhood Newspaper 122
Talking Timeline 131
The Little Library 138
Expanding Circles Social Studies Projects 142
The School of Citizens 143
Government Roles and Leadership 149
Peace, Equity and Justice 155

4 **Nature and the World: Science and Movement** 160
Philosophy and Application 160
Community Gardens 161
Ecosystem Expo 167
The Laboratory 172
Obstacle Courses and Workout World 177
Walk 'n' Talk Trail 181

5 **Working Together in the Digital World** 187
Philosophy and Application 187
Navigating Technology is Literacy 189
The Digital Classroom 190
Blended Models 192

Acknowledgements

Many thanks are in order to the community of people who have helped me throughout the process of writing this book. First thanks go out to the Kinderchat community who are some of the most dedicated, knowledgeable, and talented folks in the field. Amy Murray, Carrie Marshall and Christine Lederer are tried and true-blue colleagues that stand out with the global community of teaching and learning. Thank you also to Mardelle Sauerborn for her kind consideration of the initial outline and a huge thank you to all the many weekly moderators and guests over the years that have made Kinderchat such a special place of professional generosity and community of sharing.

Play is an incredible vehicle for learning that is often misunderstood or dismissed. I wrote this because of and for my early childhood and Kinderchat colleagues as too often the brilliant work and techniques used by educators working with the smallest learners is hidden away from the larger educational community. Children don't just miraculously stop learning from play once they turn six or seven and it is my hope that this book begins to bring that to light.

The next set of thanks go to my beloved school community. I've had the pleasure of learning and growing at Stuart Country Day School of the Sacred Heart in Princeton, New Jersey throughout my professional career. It truly is a special occurrence to have the opportunity to be a part of a community in the way that a school uniquely allows you to be. Thanks go out to all the many students, colleagues and administrators who have supported me throughout my professional journey. Special thanks go out to the Janiszewski, Toro and Badros families for allowing me to share their children's work in this book. Thank you also to my colleague Elizabeth Collins, who held my hand during the final submission process.

Thank you also to David Poras, of Mathigon.org for his efforts in helping me secure permission for the free images from Mathigon used in showcasing the math portfolios. More thanks go out to two specific teachers: Meg Leventhal, who teaches 3rd grade and to Christine Forte who teaches 6th grade science. Meg has extensive experience in Project Based Learning and serves as a professional trainer in New Jersey. While the projects contained in this book are a departure from Project Based Learning, Meg generously agreed to meet with me to share and talk. Her knowledge and insight were so impressive, and she has such a drive and passion for teaching and learning that permeates throughout her entire family and larger community. Christine Forte, who teaches 6th grade, kindly chatted with me throughout the process of writing this book about her own experiences and challenges with incorporating projects into her classroom and how she creatively pushes student thinking in her own classroom. Children are lucky that there are teachers out there like these wonderful professionals.

To my closest circle, my dear family, and friends, I thank you for keeping me laughing and for your goodness of character that I cherish. None of us is perfect, least of all me, and I am so glad we are all human in the most human of ways. I am so grateful for each one of you that I hold so dear.

Finally, though it may be a bit strange to do, I want to acknowledge myself. I never dreamed of writing books and yet here I am doing so somehow all while moving house and working full time. I am proud of my efforts and grateful for the opportunity to share my learning and teaching experiences with you, dear reader. I hope you find this book useful, or at the very least, easy, and pleasurable to read and that you use it in good faith to foster more fun and playful, deep learning experiences with your students.

Introduction and Getting Started

About Kinderchat

Kinderchat is an online educational professional group that was started in 2010 by Amy Murray and Heidi Echternacht. Over the years, educators from Canada, Jamaica, England, Northern Ireland, and the United States have led other educators in topics of conversation surrounding early childhood education. Being in regular professional dialogue with other dedicated practitioners provides teachers with key opportunities to reflect, laugh and share success stories and failures without judgment, all in service of honing their craft. It is authentic professional development, done voluntarily and without credit or compensation. Kinderchat is a labor of love that could not happen without the dedication of the moderators and participants who join in each week. This year's moderators are Heidi Echternacht from the US, Rachael McDonald from Jamaica, Amy Murray, Kathleen Ruff and Christine Lederer from Alberta, Canada, Faige Meller from California, USA, and Carrie Marshall from Prince Edward Island, Canada. (2022-2023)

Five primary goals were established at the onset of Kinderchat:

1. To facilitate discussions among educators, parents, policy makers, and the public about best practices in early childhood education
2. To create a collaborative space where teachers, administrators, parents, and organizations can share both their knowledge and the challenges of the learning and teaching of young children
3. To highlight, learn from, and discuss different philosophies of teaching and learning with young children
4. To promote real-world and real-life experiences of working daily with young children, always preserving the dignity and importance of the unique experiences of the young child and the critical nature of educating within Developmentally Appropriate Practices
5. To create a greater sense of community among those working with Young Children

For over twelve years, Kinderchat has held firm to those goals and is proud of all the work we have done to support educational practice among both pre-service and practicing educators.

So, why is this book aimed at the broader elementary school community? Because Kinderchat believes that:

- many of the unique educational practices within the early childhood setting shouldn't stop just because a child turns six, seven or seventy-seven
- learning and human development go hand in hand and that children deserve time to explore, process, fail, and explore their world and learn in ways that are meaningful and authentic
- play forms the basis of all learning and is not something frivolous or silly, but a serious and complex method of learning that deserves the respect, attention, and understanding of the larger educational community
- the depth, meaning, and quality of work many teachers are doing in the early childhood classroom is

extraordinary and deserves more attention from the world of education
♦ children can learn more content more effectively by incorporating more of the methodology and practices of the early childhood classroom into the elementary school setting.

The Goals of This Book

There are vast amounts of books available to educators that are basically tomes of rationale for "educational change". Over and over, from cover to cover, teachers are hit over the head with the need for abstract change in education. Yet, few, if any, provide the everyday teacher with the guidance and practical outline she needs to be able to incorporate more child centered, differentiated, developmental, and content rich practical projects into her curriculum while still maintaining coverage of the almighty standards. This often results in good teachers feeling both overwhelmed and lost on the highway of progressive educational methods.

Well, have no fear – Kinderchat is here! This book is born from decades of educational experience and "trying to figure it all out." Working from broad foundational experience in the early childhood setting, this book outlines the structures, philosophies, and child-centered, playful approach to learning most commonly seen in early childhood settings. The projects are designed to punctuate curriculums and enhance elementary school academic programs through real-world application. Each project takes a distinct "play approach" and illustrates how inviting play into academics forms an essential "back and forth" between application and skill development. Grounded in early childhood philosophy, this book offers a sense of discovery, playfulness, imagination, and spontaneity to elementary school academic work and subjects, while keeping skills in the foreground.

The goals of this book include:

♦ Providing multi-age and differentiated leveled experiences that help accommodate a variety of skill levels and that provide high interest learning opportunities for students

- Showcasing unique play-based, community approaches to projects designed to enhance elementary school curriculums
- Opening up early childhood learning models to elementary grade learners as essential practice for educators to incorporate more play-based experiential learning into their programs to enhance learning and sense making.

How to Use this Book

This book is meant to be more of a reference guide and map versus a step-by-step procedural manual. The projects are meant to be browsed through to find one of interest to you rather than read through in a sequential manner. While detailed "how-to" guidelines are provided, each educator will need to modify the projects to fit the setting, situation, group, and experience levels. Some of the projects outlined in this book are quite complex to pull off. Don't let that scare you. The idea is to start with a tiny seed – a small piece of the project – and then to slowly add to it as teacher and student work **TOGETHER** to create what becomes a "Play Project." In practice, these projects occur in the opposite order of "details first and understanding later" as they ask teacher and student to create and imagine first and add details as needed. The Play Projects outlined in this book should be constructed in the same spirit of architecture's Louis Henry Sullivan's mantra, "form follows function." Until something is needed by the student or scenario, don't add it. In this way, the projects become much more approachable as you gain experience and confidence.

Besides going slowly, the most important thing to know about each of the projects outlined is that **THEY ARE PLAYFUL**. Is it contradictory to say that in bold caps? It may require underlining as well as the single most detrimental factor to each of these projects is… ADULTS. No one can kill a good play scenario like an adult. The adult can be the death eater, sucking the joy and spontaneity out of the project through overdesign, overcontrol, and intervention by not allowing children enough space and time to breathe and create. Though the adult role is critical within the Play Projects, part of the difficulty of these projects is balancing the role of teachers. This is discussed in more depth in the first chapter of this book.

Finally, it is a sincere hope that these projects offer children and teachers more joy in learning and that they open up schools and education to be more willing to engage the most powerful tool at children's disposal: their imaginations.

1

Projects Philosophy, Definitions, and Structures

General Philosophies and Definitions

The New Dynamics of Teaching in the Elementary School Setting and Systemic Stress

Teaching has changed dramatically in the last ten years. In today's complex and demanding classroom setting, there is little time for variation of ever increasing prescribed and scripted curriculums. More and more, teachers have become delivery drivers for corporate curriculums rather than being granted the professional trust and creative leeway once enjoyed by the elementary school community of educators. Between increased pressures and demands from parents, policy, administrators, and colleagues teaching older grades, the elementary school teacher has morphed from what used to be a relatively carefree profession to being rated one of the most stressful. Stress has been found to be the primary driver of why so many teachers leave the teaching profession. (Diliberti, Schwartz, Grant, 2021)

> *If working with children isn't fun, who wants to do it? If the teachers are so stressed out, they are quitting, what is it doing to our youngest students- who can't quit?*

As increased demands and prescribed solutions are added onto the already full plates of schools and teachers, mechanized delivery methods and teaching practices become lifesavers for teachers drowning in demanding workloads. "Aye, apple, ah! Got it? Great! Now let's all go do a differentiated practice worksheet." The teacher quickly sorts the completed sheets into "needs more practice" or "meets or exceeds expectations" then moves the child onto the next skill ladder. Box, check, box, check, move up a rung and over three pegs to the left. Pull a focus group. The child may or may not realize or care that they are being progressed through a prescribed series of checkboxes, but make no mistake, they ARE being led through a laundry list of "skill set" checklists over which they have little to no control or say.

Meanwhile THE CHILD is largely left out of the process, simply performing skills or not, receiving pep talks about growth mindset and can-do attitudes while he sits in the back of the classroom doodling car engine designs, earnestly wanting to do his best. Maybe one day someone will throw him a bone by having him read a paragraph about a car race and he gets to answer some comprehension questions about what he read. According to the assessment rubric, he's already rated a "3" at age seven – whatever that means, he just knows it isn't good.

Somehow, once a child turns a certain age (which is getting younger and younger), the child's instinct and ability to learn vast amounts of content through play and exploration are dissolved and dismissed as a "break from learning" rather than as a valid methodology for active school learning. A doodling boy of seven becomes "off task" and primed for being flagged for attentional issues. In the minds of many, play is relegated to recess, while "learning" is completing assigned tasks and there is little to no intersection of the two. Children are expected to turn off and on between behaviors and expectations quickly, if not immediately upon request. Suddenly and miraculously, the primary learning method by which the child learned to speak, walk, and interact with others is no longer relevant as the elementary school student becomes engaged in a series of laddered lessons in which they perform, succeed, or fail.

This educational delivery method stems from the adult's mindset and conceptual understanding of "work" and "play" versus the child's mindset of curiosity, openness, and willingness to learn and explore, with little to no concept of "failure". For many adults, "learning" is something that should be difficult and unpleasant, thus preparing the child for the unpleasantness and difficulties of adult work life. While we have progressed from some of the formalities of the Victorian era, many learning routines and expectations are still deeply embedded in delivery and achievement models.

Compliance vs. Understanding

Learners who can, or are willing to, complete a series of skills and tasks progress rapidly through the maze of rewards, while others experience punishment and develop apathy within the system. Throughout the twentieth century, the acquisition of knowledge through an academic education was viewed as a competitive sport, with gamed access points granted more easily and readily to various groups depending on numerous factors including financial circumstances, gender, skin color, and family background. As we inch closer to being halfway into the twenty-first century, technology is firmly infused in every aspect of our lives, and we are finding that rank and sort methods are not as applicable, efficient, effective, or relevant when delivering information or for optimal student learning. Now, more than ever, it is essential for students to develop rapid conceptual understandings of complex systems in order to be better able to process and organize the vast amounts of information they encounter. The educational community tries to bridge skills, tasks, and understanding by working to develop student inquiry into topics of interest, to develop critical thinking, and to encourage problem-solving skills and projects.

Skills and Inquiry

In practice, using both inquiry-based and skill-based education models require a juggling act that can be exhausting and often impossible. Therefore, many in education begin to fall into camps as skill-based folks are often bewildered at the idea of a

PROCESS model and the inquiry-based folks are passionate, but equally frustrated, at the difficulty of communicating the subtleties and complexities of the inquiry method. While adults work to make sense of the teaching strategies, unit planning, curriculums, standards, and delivery methods, there remains the child, who has miraculously by the age of five become fluent in a language and engaged in representational and abstract communication and sensemaking methodologies without much, if any, explicit instruction.

While any early childhood classroom contains much of the same dynamic push and pull between skill-based and inquiry-based models, the major difference in working with children under five is that they generally don't do well attending for long amounts of time spent "listening" to adults. Two to five minutes of listening to adults is more than enough for a young child. This forces the educational model to shift to centering movement and play into the foreground of the school experience.

By age six, this child-centered, developmental model of education then completely disappears, now often at a younger and younger age. Despite findings that academically focused early childhood programs are shown to have long-term detrimental effects, (Durkin, Lipsey, Farran & Wiesen 2022), policies and programs pushing both extremes of catch-up and competitive academic preschool programs persist and the effects of stripping children and schools of play-based learning opportunities after the age of five or six remains largely unquestioned and accepted educational practice.

Make Way for Play
It is undeniable that the primary way both humans and animals initially acquire skills is through movement and playful social interactions and exchanges. Play is our most primal, foundational, and essential method of learning. Children's rapid vocabulary development increases exponentially through the dynamic exchanges of imaginative play scenarios. Make-believe with toys and representational objects stimulates children's imaginations and gives them access to recreating their world as they work to develop social and emotional regulation. In 1989, the United

Nations outlined a charter on the basic rights of children that included the right to play. Play is such a serious business that there are multiple organizations that work to raise awareness and protect this essential right for children.

This book attempts to show how educational models and practices can build on children's play and imaginations to create projects that teach children complex concepts and enhance their vocabulary and language, while helping children develop more systemic thinking and knowledge about their world. Building upon the rich teaching practices of the early childhood classroom and deep knowledge of child development, the elementary school teacher can bring more playful, interactive, enjoyable, and complex learning to life for her students with this new model of learning and teaching.

The Skill of Sensemaking

"Sensemaking" is something we often hear little of in schools as teachers and students become more and more directed towards focusing on smaller, more measurable skills, reducing the time and attention paid to the "bigger picture." Math is a perfect example of a discipline that has been deeply affected by "skills versus sensemaking" and the math community is working hard to move students from what were, in essence, teaching practices that taught students to mindlessly perform "tricks" by following procedural recipes, to working to provide students with a more thorough understanding of operations. The paradox being that once students learn the "trick" they become less able to understand the conceptual math behind the algorithm. (Lawson, Alyssa & Ayala, Brittany & Son, Ji. 2021).

> *Children become mindless after being taught algorithms and it's very hard to cure them.*
>
> *– Constance Kamii*

For most of us, there is something deeply satisfying about accomplishing a finite task, such as following a recipe from a new cookbook, completing and (hopefully enjoying) Iing enough success to move on to the next task while showing off achievement badges and well-cooked dinners along the way. The trouble with exclusively teaching and learning that way, however, is that minimizing education to a series of laddered skills ultimately narrows the scope of understanding and comprehension, resulting in learners being dependent on recipe books and not able to see or MAKE SENSE of the larger picture. Teaching children to cook by following a series of recipes may sound great at first, as making one dish from a cookbook has a high success rate. However, what does the student do when there is no recipe to follow? Have they "mastered" a cooking concept or mastered following a recipe? Did the recipe teach them how flavors go together or how different liquids react to heat or what ingredients are necessary and what they can omit? While following recipes may lead to a more immediate feeling of success, in the end, the ability to follow a cookbook of directions is not a robust enough education to learn how to be a chef.

The goal of education is to teach children how to be independent learners and how to think critically about the world around them. It is uniquely through the struggle of play and sensemaking that children can practice and develop executive functioning skills as they experience gaps in knowledge and experience. Many can "master" a skill progression and achievement model of learning, but what ultimately happens is a reduction in the ability to operate without following a "map" of predetermined outcomes, objectives, and rewards. So often we are teaching children to recall information rather than to contextualize. Procedures loom large while understanding is pushed aside, and then, because of our own lack of ability to contextualize, we often mindlessly pass the process on to batch after batch of students.

While a finite series of skill-progression, achievement-based systems may lead to varying degrees of satisfying or unsatisfying learning outcomes, what students miss out on is the opportunity to:

- think creatively, independently, and critically versus perform
- contextualize information

- find or follow their own interests and direct their own learning
- experience the opportunity to network and collaborate versus compete for resources or achievements
- see value in exploration, discovery, and underdetermined outcomes
- dive deeper into topics of interest
- regularly share and discuss their thinking logically and publicly with opportunity to engage in dynamic exchanges of ideas and information
- be flexible and adaptable in their thinking, enough to admit errors and make adjustments when learning new information
- work with others to construct and do things of real importance.

From infancy, play is the primary method in which children make sense of their world. Sadly, even many kindergartens have been stripped of their home corners, where children play and replay everyday family life. Through playing with friends and classmates, children build executive functioning, self-regulation, literacy, and social skills, but they are also "building sense" about how their home and family operates. In essence, what children are doing in imaginative play scenarios is "making sense" of their world. The traditional home corner of the kindergarten classroom has been replaced by word walls and anchor charts where children sit and practice vocabulary through isolated tasks versus having the opportunity to build vocabulary by engaging in the dynamic verbal exchanges that occur in play centers.

> *If we taught babies to talk the way that most skills are taught in school, they would memorize lists of sounds in a predetermined order and practice them alone in a closet.*
> – Linda Darling-Hammond

Critics of play in a school setting will say things like, "That's all well and good while they're young, but when they get older, they need to know x, y, z", as if the point of learning is to endlessly prepare for the next stage. While developing skills is critical work, differentiating for each student is important and perhaps specific skills can be taught through targeted group work when the skill is needed rather than becoming everyone's entire focus every school day. Additionally, play itself teaches critical lifelong cooperative skills that children need to "be prepared" for the working world.

Humans primarily develop an understanding of complex systems through EXPERIENCE. The more teachers understand human development, the process of learning, and the complex role of play, the more they gain an appreciation and understanding for what children accomplish through something they do naturally. That experience is built through playful sensemaking, where children use their imaginations in tandem with their knowledge and experiences to create, modify, and perfect recreating and replaying complex realities and systems. Is it possible for children to "make sense" of complex systems through play? Absolutely!

Topics such as economics are often reserved for a semester in high school or presented as a vocabulary list of terms to memorize. Here are several reflections from second graders who participated in a Play Project about economics with little to no direct instruction or formal lessons about economics. These quotes are the result of simply playing in a pretend town:

- "Raising the prices, instead of getting more money, you're actually losing it because the customer thinks the price is too high."
- "People who work at the bank, you have to earn money. The bank is where you can make money trades."
- "A lot of people get into fights about money."
- "As people get more money, they start bragging about their money."
- "People who are accountants, they learn how to do the taxes."
- "People only go to that one store – the big store – and other people are like, "Only one person is at my store!" and that causes problems."

- "Someone is buying something at one store and then selling it for higher prices at their store. They actually stole it from the store."

What economic concepts and principles have these children made sense of through play? *The problems they encountered during play turned into observations and they worked to solve those problems while simultaneously forming a deep understanding of economic concepts.* While these seven-year-olds gained experience working with money in the pretend town, they also developed a true SENSE of a system and topic far beyond what is normally considered possible for young children.

As our world increases in complexity, one of the skills children need most is knowledge of how to make sense of all the information thrown their way. Without the guidance and opportunity to make sense of the facts and multitude of concepts thrown at learners, children are not receiving one of the most important skills they need and deserve in order to have a full and rich education: the ability to make sense of it all. Adding projects into the curriculum is one of the ways the educational community works to address the issue of creating more autonomy and deep thinking about topics. Understanding the role of projects, what they are and how to start one is a whole other can of worms. This next section attempts to break down and define some of the many terms out there surrounding project work and inquiry-based learning.

Methods and Approaches Surrounding Project Work and Inquiry

What are "projects"? According to Lillian Katz, a renowned expert on the Project Approach, a project "is an investigation in which basic skills are used: social, emotional, literacy, math and science." Sounds simple, to the point and easy enough. So why is there often all this confusion around them? Projects can be such a wide variety of things; maybe that's why when it comes to getting going on one, things start getting murky. Projects can be:

- short-term or year-long
- whole group, small group, or done individually
- targeted towards a specific skill or towards more general content.

Many of the definitions out there will say stern things like, "projects offer rigorous learning opportunities to showcase 21st century skills." However, that's not really a definition unique to projects and does little to help anyone understand what projects are and how they uniquely function within the curriculum. Definitions like that do a lot to help muddy the waters of understanding and therefore implementation – and there are plenty of examples of that within the world of project work and education! Which is, in part, why a book like this is so necessary.

> *The Project-Based Learning (PBL) workshop I attended started off great! We educators were acting as the learners in the room, led by a presenter who was engaging and who made me eager to share this type of work with my own students. Working in groups, we completed a series of investigative activities, gathering information and then preparing to present our work. Every group seemed to have fun, each presentation was unique, and it demonstrated how PBL can be a valuable way of teaching and learning.*
>
> *Next, we entered the 'debrief' portion of the workshop, breaking down what had been done and how to re-create this in our own classrooms. The problem was, the PBL template was almost blank. There was no "How To" to instruct us on how to make this process work with our own students. I still didn't know how to start or what type of content or standard worked best when applying PBL.*
>
> *When I told the instructor that I did not know where to go from here, the response was that I should make it my own, and that the template was mainly blank intentionally. I was deflated and left feeling like the day had been a waste. I could not see a clear path and didn't know where to start.*
>
> *– Christine Forte, 6th grade, NJ*

The issue with many workshops and tutorials is that they may build understanding of technique, need, and importance, but often leave teachers unsure of where to begin with constructing their own projects. The teacher in the above scenario did manage to put together a fun and interesting project, however.

> *Having tried PBL several times now, there is one project that I like the best. The standard says that students will "Evaluate competing design solutions..." This is my favorite because I present the class with an overview of the project, and then announce that it is Opposite Day! For the duration of the project, every day students determine the worst option provided.*
>
> *We do this during our environmental science unit on human impact - so instead of selecting geothermal or hydro-electricity for example, the students will choose coal power plants. Instead of providing incentives for public transportation, the kids will create new car dealerships and remove bike lanes from the roads. The kids love this project because they try one-upping each other in the worst ways.*
>
> *– Christine Forte, 6th grade, NJ*

This next section looks at some of the definitions surrounding the inquiry method and project work. This is by no means a comprehensive list of terms you will hear swirling around out there, as the histories and comprehensive understandings of each of these terms is much more complex than what is presented here. This is simply a primer and an "untangling of terms" to help us get started.

Inquiry Method

Many in the educational field may be surprised at how few teachers are truly familiar with the inquiry method of teaching. The inquiry method is as old as Socrates and his school of philosophy and was revived into the modern system of education through the work of John Dewey. It is basically the idea of learning through questioning, with the idea being that probing dialogue helps sharpen logic and rationale as students begin to engage in deeper thought, reflection, and contemplation through conversations. Inquiry-based projects are projects that follow a group or an individual's line of questioning and wonder and where students engage in research to discover the answer or to learn what they can about the topic.

Inquiry-based teaching would be the equivalent of the "slow food movement" of the food industry. In inquiry-based learning, the role of the teacher is to offer less of an explanation of facts than it is to offer more questions designed to push student thinking. When a student observes, "The wind is blowing so hard!" Instead of offering an answer, the teacher asks questions like, *"What makes you say that? I wonder why that is. Is there a way we can find out how hard it is blowing?"* Ideally, then, students work to construct activities, experiments, and research and further develop questions in service of learning about wind. In this day and age of fast information, the development of the habit of inquiry in both teacher and student has become difficult and often a forgotten or completely ignored skill, as many teachers rush in with an answer and the wonder of it all is over before it ever begins. The biggest hurdle for teachers working to incorporate the inquiry method is learning how to be restrained enough to not offer students solutions instead of offering good questions, but to still offer instructional supports that lead to increased student knowledge and sensemaking.

In practice, the inquiry method is really hard to do. Why?

- ♦ It requires the support, buy-in and understanding of both administration and parents so that teachers can focus on the inquiry rather than defending the method.
- ♦ Inquiry is subtle, slow, and complex, which makes it difficult to explain to parents and administration whose support teachers need to sustain the method.
- ♦ People want fast food, fast learning, and quick outcomes and results and inquiry are slow and more deliberate, so the nature of the method is counteractive to our current culture.
- ♦ Inquiry takes restraint, practice, and ongoing study for teachers to get good at implementing it.

- ♦ Developing and asking good questions is a difficult skill for teachers to perfect (it takes time, attention, and effort).
- ♦ Written-out, pre-planned lesson plans that must be turned in weekly to administration make applying the inquiry method challenging.
- ♦ Students themselves may be impatient and need time and practice with the method.
- ♦ The goal is not to create a final product as much as it is to develop a "habit of mind."

For all the difficulties, however, inquiry-based learning will motivate and light up students like nothing else does within the classroom. When students are provided the opportunity to discover and lead their own learning, they become electrified and intensely motivated, especially at the elementary levels. Inquiry-based teaching and learning is something every teacher should work to gain experience with and to engage in ongoing professional dialogue and development around. It is not something easily learned and takes sustained practice to mature into the methodology, but it is an essential approach to learn more about for any teacher truly serious about developing the craft and practice of teaching.

The Project Approach

Learning and teaching through project work has a long history, with origins stretching back to apprenticeship learning, and it was reborn in the early twentieth century by educators such as John Dewey who were looking for new ways to engage learners. The Project Approach is deeply embedded within the Reggio Emilia philosophy of education. The approach is less focused on "instruction" and more focused on the process of inquiry through creating questions and documenting thoughts, observations, and, in turn, more questions.

> *Children are always learning – maybe not what you want them to learn, but they are always learning.*
>
> – *Lillian Katz*

The Project Approach:

- is often used in early childhood circles but is not a method specific to early childhood; multiple examples of projects are available for elementary school programs
- offers educators strategies and methods of investigation and documentation to begin engaging in this kind of work
- focuses on inquiry, gathering data, and documentation as primary skills
- is more straightforward in methodology and practice than many of the other methods used to explain inquiry-based learning and project work.

Lillian Katz, Ph.D. is a primary expert on the Project Approach. Extensive documentation surrounding the Project Approach is available through the Illinois Early Learning website and provides videos, guidelines, prompts, and ideas for teachers wanting to learn more about this method of teaching. A few of the projects outlined on the "Project Guides" section of the Illinois Early Learning Website are: *"Things to Sit On"*, *"Investigating Wheels"*, and *"Where Does the Water Go? Investigating Pipes and Plumbing."*

The main difficulty for teaching using the Project Approach is navigating subtle shifts in language and forming good questions. That doesn't mean the Approach is difficult and therefore flawed, but it is a reason why some teachers and systems may avoid investing time and attention to a serious study of the method.

Some tips and quotes from Lillian Katz on formulating questions to drive inquiry learning are:

- "Always ask "what makes you think so?" vs "how do you know?"
- "Ask, "what are some foods you don't like" vs "your favorite."
- "What don't you like about them?"

- "Which foods can be eaten raw? Have to be cooked? Mashed? Ground? Stirred? Steamed? What gets soft when it's cooked? Changes color? What goes in a can? Box? Jars? Cartons? How many kinds of cereal are in your house?"

  – *Lillian Katz, Ph.D.*

You can learn more about Lillian Katz and the Project Approach through the Illinois Early Learning website at https://illinoisearlylearning.org/resources/blogs/perspectives/ and through Sylvia Chard's work at Duke University at https://www.projectapproach.org.

Conferences Supporting the Project Approach

One of the most fun methods used to metacognitively explain inquiry and the project method is the annual *Constructing Modern Knowledge* conference, created by Gary Stager, Ph.D. He challenges teachers to create, tinker, play, and invent using computers and various tools in a three-day workshop model that brings in well-known speakers and experts in the field. An expert in the Reggio method of education, Gary Stager's work and workshops should not be missed by anyone wanting to do serious work within the realm of inquiry and project-based learning and teaching. His website contains treasure troves of articles, resources, history, research, and writing about multiple topics within the arena of project work and inquiry learning. You can read more and discover multitudes of resources on his website, http://professorgarystager.com/.

Constructivism and Constructionism

Just to maximize confusion, here are these two similarly named terms, with subtle differences, meanings, and intentions! Yay! Who said the world of education isn't fun?! It is! Here we go:

Constructivism:
- is a theory of how knowledge is constructed, developed by Jean Piaget, with work of Dewey, Vygotsky and Jerome Bruner, and many others offering supporting theories of constructivism.

- views learning as a social, individual, natural, and dynamic process.
- operates from the basis that knowledge is constructed within the stages of development:
  - assimilation = "this small flying thing is a bee"
  - accommodation = "not all small flying things are bees".
- believes that experiences, especially social experiences, are the primary drivers of learning and knowledge constructs.

Constructionism:
- is a theory based on constructivism, developed by Seymour Papert, who was a mathematician who worked with Jean Piaget.
- primarily focuses on computers, engineering, and math, though is applicable to other disciplines.
- proposes "problem-based" learning where students are given real-world problems to solve and they then work to create, solve, and debug solutions.
- is based on the idea that people learn primarily by constructing things.

Each of these theories holds a key place within the realm of teaching through project work, as they focus on how learning occurs and on methods of how to support student learning. Constructivism provides theoretical foundational support for inquiry-based learning and projects, while constructionism provides a computerized blueprint (that you must make yourself, of course!)

So, now that we have constructivist foundational support and constructionist blueprints, we are next offered a framework.

Understanding by Design

Understanding by Design is a framework for lesson, unit, and curricular project planning and design, developed and trademarked by Grant Wiggins and Jay McTighe. The "UbD" system:

- formulates design by focusing on desired outcomes and understandings first, rather than focusing on activity planning first
- focuses on the importance of having a central question is at the core of the course and all projects and activities are done in service of the question
- ensures that all assessment outcomes and rubrics are created before activities are planned
- provides a step-by-step handbook and outline with templates for how to design lessons, projects and units.

Understanding by Design takes the same question as mentioned in the previous section on inquiry, "*Where does the wind come from?*", and offers educators structural planning around that question. Desired outcomes are planned first with rubrics providing clear maps for students to be able to demonstrate and measure what successful projects look like. Lessons and activities are then planned in service of the question and desired outcomes. Assessment focuses on having students demonstrate proficiency by being able to transfer what they learned into real-world scenarios and performance tasks. The idea of "transfer" is key here, as the goal of Understanding by Design is to create projects where the student applies their new skills and knowledge outside of the project and into more learning experiences.

While there are definitely plenty of gems to discover here and many curricular and project-based units are designed by using this model, overall, it can be a difficult and complex approach to execute well. Sometimes, the methodical planning and trying to "do it right" can overtake the entire project, to the point where the teacher has lost enthusiasm before the project ever starts. Additionally, some of the assessment tasks ask students to create things such as a diary detailing what their life might have been like living within a period of history, or they may ask them to describe how to tile a bathroom floor using mathematical concepts and skills. While these may sound interesting, in practice, elementary school students, even with sustained support, often have little construct of where to begin with those types of overwhelming projects and so are highly prone to failing to measure up to the desired outcome. Even with the difficulties, it is a design framework worthy of teachers' attention and study, as Understanding by Design aims to keep a driving question and transfer goals at the forefront of quality project design.

You can find out more about UbD from several resources and videos online, through the Authentic Education website https://authenticeducation.org/about-authentic-education/ or at Jay McTighe's website https://jaymctighe.com/ which has numerous resources on Project Based Learning presented here: https://jaymctighe.com/wp-content/uploads/2022/02/Project-based-Websites-2.10.22-1.pdf

How to PBL

With all these terms now in place, how do you take them and create a project for students? Enter the term "Project Based Learning." There are so many books on project-based learning, many of which complicate the method with elaborate design templates to the point of muddying the waters. After filling out fifteen pages of planning materials, you can often forget what you are even trying to do.

In a nutshell:

1. Start with a question or problem.
   Most every method seems to agree on starting with a KWL style topic web as a starting point. What do we know (K), wonder, or want (W) to know and reflect on what we learned (L)? Basically, collectively brainstorm and list everything we know about the topic and revisit that regularly. Goals and skills should be clearly outlined for students before the project begins so that they know markers and indicators of a good project.
2. Inquiry, Research, Lessons, and Activities
   Students choose an angle of investigation, collect data, conduct research, and interview experts; student inquiry

is supported with lessons and activities in service of the question to construct knowledge around the topic.
3. Present work
   Students publicly present their findings or the solution to the problem that they worked to solve. Apply a rubric for performance assessment, reflective of goals and skills.

The company PBLWorks, formerly the Buck Institute of Education, provides PBL training, books, and resources for a fee. Their website is https://www.pblworks.org/.

Activities vs. Project-Based Learning

In many cases, much of the misunderstanding around PBL exists in the difference between activities and projects. Basically, the difference between activities and projects is:

- ♦ Activities place learning goals as secondary and are often done in service of the theme. "Let's make something, learn some fast facts and have a parade." The craft and the parade are the driving force, and the learning goals are secondary. While activities support projects, they are not the project themselves.
- ♦ Projects attempt to be more focused on academic skills and content in service of a question. "What are some similarities and differences between "X" and "Y"? The investigation is the driving force. The learning goal and question is central. A parade may happen but it's celebratory versus the main point of the project.

Observations from in the Field

While there are many examples of exceptional PBLs out there, there are also many issues that come up, such as:

- ♦ Basing the entire project on a question puts a lot of pressure on forming the right question. Asking a good question can be extremely difficult, so much so that the entire project can go bust if that question isn't shaped properly.
- ♦ At times there can be an overabundance of planning and performance tasks surrounding the learning goals,

but the learning activities do not necessarily address the topic in meaningful ways.
- Many projects are not developmentally appropriate for students. While tiling bathroom floors and creating blueprints for clients in need of a home are lofty goals and it's easy to see the mathematical applications within, they are projects that require a level of skill that many nine or even twenty-nine-year-olds may not have. It's not that kids can't do hard things; it's more a case of setting kids up for failure by asking them to construct things that aren't accessible or doable within a reasonable level of attainment.
- Many of the final projects are clearly done with parental assistance and still end up being "science fair" type projects where the presentations do not reflect the actual work or learning that took place. Professionals familiar with authentic children's work can easily spot an adult's hand in final presentations. There are numerous examples of final projects clearly done either with a craft recipe type of approach or done with a great deal of assistance from adults.
- Much of the verbiage and planning structures for teachers are overwrought and difficult to follow and use. At times it seems as if project planning has been maximized for a manufactured type of complexity over clarity. Overburdening projects with detailed and elaborate planning templates can result in teachers avoiding them altogether.
- Assessment within the elementary school setting should not be overburdened by elaborate performance ratings of children's learning efforts. Ongoing individual dialogue and regular feedback combined with "checklists for success" can help ensure that children begin to self-check their work and to know what a successful project looks like.

The Play Projects

"Knowledge is a consequence of experience"
– Jean Piaget

What are "Play Projects"?

Increasingly, elementary school has become a push down of skills, concepts, and curriculum from middle and high school as they struggle to keep up with the demands they face. Too often, elementary school teachers are asked to place overly complicated and non-developmentally-appropriate structures and demands upon their students in service of endlessly "preparing" children for the "next step" in their education. As a result, there can be an overabundance of planning activities and a shortage of experiential learning opportunities. This can often result in children "checking out" emotionally and mentally, as school can leave them behind at younger and younger ages.

"Play Projects" are projects that build on a child's natural developmental stages from the ground up as they attempt to create and simulate real world scenarios for children to "play at" various realities in order to gain understanding. They are meant to be "serious fun" where learners become deeply engaged in projects and activities that have meaning, consequence, and impact.

Drawing deeply on Piagetian principles of knowledge acquisition, Play Projects are not project based in the "traditional" sense. While they are projects, they focus more on embedding the process of inquiry into the fabric of the experience through play. Play Projects are wholly experiential, with the outcome being knowledge acquisition through sensemaking. The vehicle for the projects is play and there's no one particular "driving question", but rather multitudes of questions, problems, experiences, and continuous feedback that all arise freely, naturally, frequently, and spontaneously.

Much like the "housekeeping corner" in the early childhood classroom, Play Projects are focused on promoting sensemaking of the larger world by building and developing the learner's inquiry level through actual experiences. Learning occurs within and because of the playing. Experiential and constructivist in nature and design, the "Play Project" approach to teaching and learning as outlined in this book stems directly from practices common in the early childhood setting where children learn primarily through experiential centers designed to maximize play.

The idea of Play Projects came very naturally to me after years of working in the early childhood setting where whole worlds of imagination were constructed and reconstructed daily. Play Projects were born by watching children play and wanting to enhance their play by adding interesting materials and providing academic structures where and when it became applicable. I found myself feeling that my best teaching was occurring when I had simply become the "supply lady" during playtimes. After play sessions, we would discuss and reflect as a group what was happening. When I moved into teaching in the elementary grades, I found teaching through play continued to be a highly successful and effective method to help students make sense of complex concepts.
– Heidi Echternacht

Imagine the difference in the experiences of nine-year-olds "learning about banking" and "playing bank." Approaching the project through a traditional PBL lens might involve:

1. Question: What role do banks play in the community?
2. Create: Brainstorm/KWL/topic web: "What we know about banks"
3. Activities: research/videos/reading/vocabulary/working with money
4. Field trip to a local bank
5. Student poster presentations about role of banks in community

Whereas, if you want to start "playing bank", you immediately jump into the action, but questions quickly pop up, such as:

1. What kinds of materials do we need to gather?
2. What kinds of things do we do here?
3. What are some roles and jobs within the bank?
4. What logistical problems are we having? How can we solve them?
5. How can we streamline our play systems to be more efficient?
6. Why is this place important to the classroom community?

Note that you can do all the things listed in the PBL along with the play version, but PBL rarely, if ever, includes aspects of the play version of the project. Would a PBL inquiry unit on banking ever yield a discussion of the importance of work shifts? Would students be able to provide detailed job descriptions and share how they solved and dealt with specific problems and challenges? Would students be able to provide detailed explanations of the importance of accuracy in spreadsheets and accounting? Could they explain how credit cards are representational currency? Could they explain interest rates? Talk about transfer goals! Children can do and learn all these things almost effortlessly through the language of experiential learning called "play". There is a massive difference in children reading about those things and experiencing them firsthand.

Where Project-Based Learning is based on one question and performing skills and completing activities in service of that question, Play Projects are focused on generating many questions and active problem solving through an organic inquiry process. As problems and conflicts arise, children work to find solutions and conversations and dialogue reflect on that process. Where feedback is planned in Project-Based Learning, feedback within the Play Projects is happening constantly and becomes part of the "lesson" as teacher and students work in tandem to create real simulations and scenarios. Only through the experience of "working" in a bank can children begin to construct a genuinely authentic idea of how to "Describe the role of banks in an economy" or "Describe the role of other financial institutions in an economy" – as are two standards outlined in the National Council for Social Studies in the C3 Framework – otherwise it is simply an exercise in reading comprehension.

While you can take children methodically through a study of banks and money systems and ask them to theoretically design their own system, what does it accomplish? Kids are initially going to be very excited that they get to DO SOMETHING but then become overloaded and disappointed as they realize the magnitude of the task, which actually sets them up for failure in the first place. Kids need structures to work within and, without the experience, they are simply reciting or recounting what they've read or researched. The act of playing and working in a bank, done in conjunction with reading about and researching money and banks, yields a much richer knowledge building and learning experience.

The Play Projects listed in this book are scaffolded to provide a wide range of skill development and are outlined with the necessary time frames, materials, goals, difficulty levels, preparation, layout and design, scaffolding, integrations, outcomes, assessments, troubleshooting, and resources. Each project in this book focuses on:

- fostering cross curricular connections to help streamline a curriculum to do "double duty" by achieving multiple goals and standards within one project, thus creating *more time* within the day.
- playful, experiential, developmentally appropriate and community-based approaches to teaching academic subjects.
- how to design larger scale school-wide projects that reinforce concepts and skills taught in elementary school academic programs, taking some of the weight off individual classroom teaching and into community based "process circles".

One of the big differences between the projects outlined in this book and many project based approaches is that these projects do not involve asking children to examine one specific question before starting the project. Instead, questions are peppered in and posed constantly by both teacher and student throughout and may be answered as they situationally arise. Through regular group inquiry, reflection and observations, students notice patterns in the play and share their thinking. While questions like, "What businesses are essential to towns?" or "How do banks exchange money?" may occur, the driving force of the project is not in service of an essential question but rather for students to acquire knowledge and make sense of the system.

Another major difference is that unless the project is specifically a "design and make" type of project, the Play Projects are not asking students to spend lots of time in the "makerspace design" department producing craft products like logos, diaries, dioramas, or miniature houses as part of a learning activity. Activities such as making historical diaries and designing logos often lead to children spending lots of time designing the physical look of the project and engaging in endless amounts of planning. Very often these types of creations end up becoming symbolic products that dance around the concept rather than help forward the construction of knowledge and sensemaking for the student. Instead, the Play Projects are asking students to engage in play – and therefore, problem solving – in service of creating real-world, open-ended experiences and simulations that directly impact and transfer to greater sensemaking abilities for students.

Why Play?
Play is something children generally know how to do with little to no "instruction." While some children do need guidance with learning to play and may struggle for various reasons, most elementary aged children are skilled enough to know that play is an open ended, dynamic, imaginative world that is spontaneously constructed with little to no guidance from adults. When you climb in and operate from the position of the mind of a child, play is a vast world of endless exploration. It is never work or laborious because the world of play is constantly filled with possibility and imagination. There may be roadblocks, arguments, and disruptions, but the child's hunt for adventure and imaginative connection with the world perseveres.

> *Every elementary school teacher should be prepared and qualified to talk about how the rich world of play directly contributes to a child's ability to learn, cooperate, and develop intellectually, socially and emotionally.*
> – Heidi Echternacht

Kinderchat dedicated an entire chapter to play in the book "The Kinderchat Guide to the Classroom" and there are additional resources listed for you at the end of this chapter if you are looking for more information on the importance of play in children's learning. In short, the key importance of play is that it is the primary method by which children develop self-regulation and language skills as they interact dynamically with each other, all while engaged in real-world problem solving. Play is children working to negotiate the subtleties of social dynamics in the pursuit of creating something together, whether that be a show, store, club, or invention.

Immediately, some adults will balk at the term "play", which is, in many minds, something reserved for young children and not related to school learning in the least. For many adults, learning should not be fun and if it is fun, then it is not learning. They will tell you things like "nine-year-old children are too old to learn through play", "they are bored by it", "they are ready for more" or they will say that it is not "rigorous enough" as a method of building knowledge. Each of these statements shows a lack of experience and depth of understanding about how play is a unique and essential component of how humans learn. Make-believe and pretend play are highly engaging methods of learning and provide some of the most "rigorous" critical thinking skills for children as they begin to make sense of the world. The highest forms of play are within art, music, theater, and language, as well as math and science. When you can play with a topic, it is a demonstration of deep understanding and knowledge. Play is also a vehicle that can help children understand complex topics well beyond the typical expectation for elementary-school-aged children.

Without going into a lengthy rationale for the value and essential role of play in human learning for doubtful adults, for our purposes here, using the term "simulations" may ease immediate defenses and protestations. Whatever the term, when we are engaged in creating and playing out scenarios, we seek to create evermore "real-er" experiences. The desire and hunt for authenticity in the play, or simulation, helps inform and refine the work, while providing automatic wormholes and avenues for research, investigation, and inquiry. Absent of play, or EXPERIENCE, we are often asking children to think academically about topics they know absolutely nothing about.

Where adults talk and plan, children play. Children need and want to learn by getting right into the doing, not endlessly preparing and planning for the doing. In the elementary school setting, there is often an abundance of examples where children (and teachers!) are engaged in overplanning and underplaying. While you can make children sit and create elaborate plans, when the "doing" starts, those plans quickly change and often evaporate. It's not the planning that matters as much as the reflection of the process that matters. From the reflection, new plans emerge, change, and inform the child's experience.

What is Play?

Strangely, for something so primal and innate, few educators and adults would be able to provide a complete definition of the term "play." In an article entitled "The Value of Play I: Definitions of Play Gives Insights" (2008), Peter Gray, Ph.D., and author of the book "Free to Learn" (2013), defines play:

> *Play is self-chosen and self-directed. Play is activity in which means are more valued than ends. Play has structure, or rules, which are not dictated by physical necessity but emanate from the minds of the players. Play is imaginative, non-literal, mentally removed in some way from "real" or "serious" life. Play involves an active, alert, but non-stressed frame of mind.*

Becoming well voiced in the practice of play is essential professional development in working to apply and perfect teaching techniques of the projects in this book. Teachers should stand back and observe, not in a policing way, but in a "what can I learn from watching these children play?" way.

Being a Professional in "Play Mode"

Some teachers may struggle to find a professional level of balance between being "silly", joking and having fun with their students and then being able to turn that off and turn on teacher mode. Other teachers may be forgetting to enjoy a moment of less seriousness with their students and to engage with them occasionally in a playful, relaxed way. While most teachers, students,

TABLE 1.1 Table distinguishing between "Play" and "Not Play."

Play	Not Play
Children have free choice to make decisions and drive the action.	Assigned to centers, children must complete an activity or spend a required amount of time in the center.
Children's use of materials is free flowing and can change rapidly. Baskets can become hats.	Teacher: "We aren't using that basket as a hat. Put it down; it is a basket." Teacher controls the materials.
Children co-create the rules. Rules often change on the fly as the situation varies.	Extensive directions in the center. The child is not driving the action but following adult-created rules and procedures.
Children's voices are heard most.	Adult voices are heard most.
Adults may seem "unaware", but are actually very aware, observant of play and may participate when/if invited. Teachers are used by children as resources and consultants.	Adults are patrolling and policing and primarily concerned with maintaining order. Teachers show children how to use the center "properly".

and classrooms have achieved some level of "knowing of each other", fostering play within a classroom is a practice that can take some doing for those unaccustomed to the practice.

There's a wide world of difference between "instructing" children and being able to get on the floor and play WITH a group of children. If you've ever spent any time with children, after a careful looking-over and assessment by the children, as an adult, you may occasionally be deemed interesting enough to receive an invitation to play. The younger the child, the more frequently you may encounter these types of unspoken invitations where a child offers you a tasty rock cookie or pretend piece of cake. Adults generally know that you humbly accept the treat with a smile, pretend to eat it, and return it to them enthusiastically declaring, "Delicious! The best I've ever had! Thank you!" It is the test of a gift and most every child gives it at some point to an adult.

This invitation speaks a great deal to relationship building; as play is one of a child's primary ways of communicating, you as a professional should know how to speak the language.

While it is not necessary or even preferred for teachers to insert themselves into the action of play, being playful while being a professional can be more difficult for some than others. Some adults may mistakenly view play as a license to be silly, rather than to show how to respectfully engage in a play scenario. Other teachers may feel detached from play and unable to connect with their students. Whatever the extreme, striking a balance and being experienced in managing and observing children at play is something every teacher of elementary-school-aged children should be prepared to do well. Children are always looking to adults for guidance and any elementary school teacher should be able to engage in some degree of healthy professional play.

The Importance of Co-Creation: Cooperation and the Collective
Many people might be very surprised at the skill and talent fostering play takes. Co-creating a play scenario requires a delicate hand, as play requires a degree of unexpectedness and lots of spontaneity. In a scenario of starting to "play bank", it might mean that an area of the classroom suddenly appears with some materials left about, including play money and coins. To get things started, the teacher might suddenly overhear a few children talking about the materials and listen for a spark that can ignite into a banking center. Or maybe it begins by just casually asking around if anyone can deposit the play money the teacher is holding into an account. Someone will inevitably come to the teacher's assistance as they recognize that it is really an invitation to play, and someone will gladly accept the teacher's invitation. However you begin, it should always be the children's spark of an idea; with the teacher simply providing the wood and working together, that spark slowly builds into a fire. To foster co-creation, the teacher's primary role is to set the stage and create space for play, to step back and observe, and to make space and take time for reflection and feedback.

As the play bank scenario begins to take hold, children immediately start operating from a place of critical thinking, problem solving, and engineering. What's an account? It doesn't matter for now, watch the student switch into play mode instantly and say with a knowing smile, "Yes, I can take care of that for you, ma'am, it'll just be a moment." Instant buzz. Suddenly, though no one really knows what it means, everyone wants an account. Soon word spreads quickly as to what an account is without any formal lesson or instruction. The teacher listens and observes the play, providing the new bankers with materials as needed to sort and store all the accounts that have now miraculously appeared. Everyone wants a turn, arguments start up, and someone comes up with the idea of working in shifts. They get busy organizing a schedule and BOOM, we have a bank manager. Problems are solved fast, on the fly, and as they arise.

Because the students know the teacher has provided the invitation to play, kids get to WORK, spontaneously constructing, imagining, and cooperating. The teacher might then drop a few good questions into the mix WHILE and AS the scenario is evolving. Soon enough you are all talking about why physically storing and carrying around coins is such a problem, as they keep spilling out of the containers and Marcus lost track of the money in Josie's account and she's mad. Is there an easier way to store the money? How can we keep better track of people's accounts? Can anyone think of a different way to keep track of coins other than by using physical coins? Real problems rapidly inspire real solutions as the form and function of play and knowledge begin to work in tandem in service of creating the most real play experience possible.

As the teacher:
- Observe the problems and allow time for solutions to naturally arise. Arguments and disagreements about the process will occur. Lean into those as they provide key social-emotional learning opportunities.
- Mirror and share your observations through regular class discussions. Document the thinking of the children's observations during discussions.
- Encourage children to create diagrams, lists, organizational charts, and plans and to keep records of their own questions.
- Allow the play scenario time and space to breathe and take on life while feeding it through materials that enhance the play.

- Observe more than you participate.
- Continue recording what happened, what questions came up, and what problems were solved.
- Support and deepen the authenticity of the play to the point where the children have gained enough EXPERIENCE to be able to showcase their reflections of the play scenario through photographs, a written or oral recounting, portfolio, or presentation.

What Kills a Good Project

As an educator, YOUR approach to projects, especially projects that incorporate play, matters. If you are too rigid, the project will die – this is 100% guaranteed. If the project is too loose, things could spiral out of control and the point is lost to mayhem. The short story to the question, "What kills a good project?" is YOU. Here are some things that can kill a good project:

- **Rigidity:** It's their project, not yours. It's OK if they don't use the materials in the way you planned. Don't introduce the project with lengthy rules and regulations about how it is supposed to work. If you start to feel children fatigue, it's generally because you've introduced too many rules and specifics about how it's "supposed to" work and not allowed enough space for their ideas to take hold. Your role is to observe rather than regulate.
- **Over-planning:** Teachers may over-plan for things they don't need and under-plan for things they don't realize they need. This is why starting small and growing into each of the projects is so important. Know where you are going but be open to lots of different ways of getting there.
- **Inexperience:** Teachers need to be experienced in the language of play and be ready and able to discuss, foster, and value its unique role in learning.
- **Lack of structure:** On the opposite end of rigidity is not providing enough structure and boundaries for children to feel safe enough to let go of having to worry about holding the whole system together and instead be able to

be free from worry, enough to create and engage in imaginative play. Children need to be provided with enough structure to feel safe and relaxed enough to play.
- Translations: As the Play Projects are so heavily process-based and the experiences are dynamic, projects can easily be dismissed as "we played bank" rather than truly reflective of the complexity of what actually happened during play. This is why documentation is such a key component to each project and why having regular class conversation and student reflections are so important.

Finally, one of the most difficult and yet rewarding challenges within a project is letting go. Once play has taken hold and you stand back watching the tornado of social-emotional and academic learning occurring, enjoy that sweet moment where you realize that you somehow managed to not kill it, but rather brought it to life.

Fostering Cross-Curricular Connections

Creating projects with multiple points of cross-curricular connections is the pinnacle of a great project and is seriously underrated and underused as a vital approach to teaching and learning in the school setting. While aligning full curriculums can be difficult and challenging to achieve, projects are smaller in scale and time commitments, so it can be an accessible way to achieve multiple curricular learning goals and objectives under one umbrella project. Create a series of spirals throughout various grades and within disciplines, carefully mapped and tracked so as to not overload any one class or system too much.

As a teacher looking to implement a cross-curricular project, the first thing you need to have is a willing colleague. You can start with the two of you hatching up a project, or begin with the project first and see what other subjects or teachers would be the most logical fit. Many people approach projects saying something like, "Let's all brainstorm and make something together." While that can work in some cases, the trouble is that large amounts of broad discussion and general planning can take up the entire life and energy of the project before it is even off the ground. For this reason, if you have something already in mind, map out your idea first and then approach your colleagues. Once they see where you are coming from, they'll be able to talk with you and see how you can work together, or not.

Sometimes the problem with collaborating with another teacher becomes that it is easy to spin off into more activity types of thematic-based teaching. This is what many of the frameworks available out there are trying to combat, but they often end up making things more complex than needed. Keep focused on what skills you are trying to get students to apply and use and keep asking, "What will students be able to have a better sense of after this project?" The pursuit of authenticity in recreating play scenarios often helps keep those questions automatically embedded into the process of the projects.

Finally, one of the most essential components of a project is communication. Poor communication can cause misunderstandings and derail a great experience. For this reason, decide on a planning platform and keep it transparent so your colleagues can see and know how the project is evolving. In this way, even hesitant contributors can find a way they can participate in, or at least be aware of, the planning and project documentation.

Digital Tools to Foster Collaboration

Working digitally is an effective way to communicate big ideas quickly to lots of people. The trouble with many digital tools within education is, again, that word, "sensemaking", as many educators struggle to place digital applications in the larger context of utility. "Working Together in a Digital World", Chapter Five of this book, talks more in detail about platforms and methods to make project collaboration work more smoothly. For now, here are some methods and applications that may be helpful:

- ♦ Create project maps to begin to share learning goals and the various discipline components.
- ♦ Use Google Sites to outline and design projects, much as you would a folder or binder.

- Plug Padlets in as tools for creating timelines, digital book bins, and video collections.
- Use Google Slides as an interactive tool for resources and student access.

You don't need to have everything "done" and then start the project. While not ideal, it's OK to still be building part of the boat as you are rowing it. Most teachers are used to that! It can even be helpful as you begin to truly co-construct the project with students. Maintain focus on what skills and knowledge you intend your students to come away with and keep rowing. Contrary to most everything in education written today, it doesn't have to be perfect; it's a process and it's OK to not do it perfectly the first time or even the third time.

Getting Started

1. Map it

The best way to get started is to think about what your students are interested in and what they want to play and talk about. Watch and listen to them and pull from their interests. Then think about your curricular goals and standards and where one can overlap the other. Once you have a spark of an idea, begin to work on a project map, pulling and blocking out academic standards and how they can fit together with the project. Don't become too obsessed with detail, as you should consider your first year of the project a launch year. Know that it might take two to three years of repeating a project to get it running seamlessly. Give yourself permission to start small and build up.

2. Design the functioning space

The next piece of the project is to design the physical space. This is as important as any setting is to any good story, and a good project is a type of learning story you are weaving together and creating with your students. Take time to think about how the students will move through the project: what will they be doing, how, and when? The early childhood setting does a remarkable job at this, as it is customary for numerous children to be using a room in multiple different ways simultaneously. Research and learn from the way early childhood educators utilize classrooms. The Kinderchat Guide to the Classroom discusses classroom design philosophy extensively and can be a useful resource for those looking to learn more. Build out centers and focus on areas of the project that can function alongside each other simultaneously. For example, the Banking project slowly expands to include an investment center across the "street." Each project in this book talks about the materials and space needs as well as spending time scaffolding how each project can unfold slowly, over time.

3. Gather resources and create platforms for documentation and research

Finally, work to create your platforms for collaboration, research, resources, and documentation. How will you be documenting student work and discussions? What resources do you need to gather beforehand? This can, and should, take most of your planning time. Gathering materials and resources also provides you with time to research, read, and imagine. While you can, and should, think of the pie-in-the-sky ultimate project, try to prevent distraction and tangents by continually circling back to refocus and center yourself on the ultimate learning goals for students. Also, while it can be difficult to be prepared for projects to go into areas you don't expect, it is key to stay open to possibilities you haven't thought of by not being rigid or too particular in the planning of how materials are to be used by students.

Assessments: Documentation, Portfolios and Forms

It's hard not to notice that anytime assessment comes up, people get intense. The temptation to wield power over another human being and judge their performance, quality, or product is a magnetic pull into the depths of human psychology. It has been ingrained in us that ranking and filing children is essential to their learning process, when in reality, there are well recognized detrimental effects. The allure is so strong that we rationalize away the harmful effects in service of appearing to be a "rigorous educational program" that is "no nonsense" in order to "prepare children for the future." While those scare tactics may work for some learners, one of the wonderful things about elementary-school-aged students is that they haven't learned to be scared of grades yet and largely still actually enjoy learning for learning's sake. On the whole, elementary-aged children generally want to do right and succeed, learn, and impress their teachers and caregivers.

The question we need to be asking is, "How (and why) should humans show evidence of their learning?" The myth of "mastery learning" stems from an idea that skill learning is finite and is something that can be "completed." However, when you look at one of the simplest mathematical concepts, counting from the number one to the number two, there is, in fact, an infinite amount of numbers in between, to the point where, in a way, you can never truly "master" counting from one to two. While you can achieve various levels of competency, proficiency, and expertise, the idea of "mastery" is largely an illusion that insists that knowledge is both finite and conquerable. In reality, knowledge is rarely, if ever, truly complete. The more you know, the more you realize you don't know. The point of learning is always to keep learning.

Once safely entangled in the web of grades and rubrics, many may spend more time gaming the system of assessment than it would take to learn the material. Students create elaborate systems of mental gymnastics to weigh and measure minimal learning efforts in proportion to the maximum grade. The learning has ceased to matter because it is the grade achievement that comes to matter.

Recognizing the importance of nurturing young children's interest in learning and school for the sake of learning is paramount to democracy and education. Rather than performing to avoid "getting in trouble", students' interests, thoughts, and insights need to be heard and valued. It is important for children to learn to modify their thinking when faced with new information and to not be fearful of punishment or shame when doing so. Educators need to look towards the elementary school model as a way they can motivate and entice learners each day without elaborate systems of rewards and punishments. Whether you decide to use grading rubrics or not, the beauty of the project model unfolds through the reflection of the experience, as those needing or wanting to add rubrics or grades can still do so through the student's individual written reflection of the project.

For each of the Play Projects listed in this book, the students' own reflection of the play experience provides the data and documentation of learning through their writing. Through conversation, documentation, portfolio presentation, and writing, students reflect on their experience to show the learning that took place. The assessment is in no way a final product of the learning but is treated as an essential piece of the learning. In this way, students and teachers co-create a body of work that directs and supports student learning goals within academic content. The goal of most every assessment presented in this book is to have students provide a written reflection about what they learned, what they made sense of, and what they still wonder.

For many, written pieces can seem daunting – especially for those working with young children. Writing was found to "reliably enhance learning in all areas" (Graham, 2020) and is woven throughout each of the Play Projects to both enhance sensemaking and serve as a reflection of the child's own progress and learning. When presented all together, the work forms both a collective and individual portfolio, while authentically embedding writing and literacy into each project.

- ◆ Collective conversations can form the backbone of a written record of young children's observations and insights and can serve to enhance perspectives for older students.
- ◆ Conduct interviews and regularly collect quotes and thinking from students during play times.
- ◆ Take photographs of the work students are doing to help serve as documentation.
- ◆ Younger children can draw and label, sequence the "how-to" steps of a project, and provide adults with guided tours and explanations of the project.

♦ Older elementary grade students complete ongoing short written pieces that share their thinking of the project along the way, with their final reflection submitted as their assessment piece.

When beginning any of the projects outlined in this book, it may take a few years of practice to fully layer in a robust portfolio system. Done carefully, with regularity, support, and practice, it becomes a much less daunting task that is very approachable, though worth serious study, as the simplicity of reflective practice is deceptive in its complexity, for both teacher and student. To start out, begin slowly with student written reflections and go from there. Each Play Project outlined in this book contains a section on assessment to help you begin to integrate the practice of reflection and documentation within each project.

While Chapter Five of this book goes into deeper detail, here are some quick tips for creating portfolio assessments and presentations:

♦ Document the entire project through photographs of the children's WORK rather than their smiling faces.
♦ Take regular notes and pull quotes from group conversations.
♦ Incorporate group documentation along with individual student documentation to provide a larger picture of the project in combination with the student's own reflections.
♦ Create timelines and deadlines for yourself and students to regularly add documentation.

Finally, and most importantly, with full awareness and admitted fear, it is assured that someone out there will try to rate and rubric children's play. Please do not do that to children, to play or to these projects. Maybe the absurdity of assessing play is why it has been eradicated from children's schooling experiences. When tempted to do so, return instead to evaluating your own ability to recognize and define play. As play, by definition, is something "done freely and without a prescribed outcome", children should never be rated or graded on their abilities.

Students don't have to participate; they can watch, they can read a book, and they can also still make astute observations and offer insights while they are engaged in other things. While some children will surely need assistance and encouragement navigating the social-emotional conflicts that may arise, each of these Play Projects offers them support by giving them time to practice and engage in developing those problem-solving skills.

Assessment Q & A:

- *So, how will children be motivated to become better?* Return again and again to the definition of play. Play is self-motivating and fulfilling. If the project is no longer playful or interesting, let it sit and come back to it later. Regular reflection and individual conversations and transparency of your "noticings" do a lot to mirror and share expectations to students. Feedback is happening all the time within the play.
- *How will we know what they learned?* Through ongoing conversations and documentation along with their written reflection.
- *What are the goals and expectations?* For students to develop and increase sensemaking about various systems and topics through play and continuous reflection.
- *What specific skills will students develop through Play Projects?*
    - Greater executive functioning and self-regulation
    - Active problem solving
    - Sensemaking skills specific to the project
    - Greater social and emotional wellbeing
    - Leadership skills
    - Critical thinking through the process of play, observation, and reflection
    - More cooperation with peers
    - Less shame around making errors and greater ability to be more mentally flexible
    - Content knowledge specific to the project
    - Motivation and excitement for learning
    - Reading and research skills

♦ Improvements in writing, vocabulary and language through ongoing, high frequency exposure, practice, and usage

References

Diliberti, Melissa Kay, & Heather, L. *Schwartz, and David Grant, Stress Topped the Reasons Why Public School Teachers Quit, Even Before COVID-19*. Santa Monica, CA: RAND Corporation, 2021. https://www.rand.org/pubs/research_reports/RRA1121-2.html.

Durkin, K., Lipsey, M. W., Farran, D. C., & Wiesen, S. E. (2022). Effects of a statewide pre-kindergarten program on children's achievement and behavior through sixth grade. *Developmental Psychology*, 58(3), 470–484. https://doi.org/10.1037/dev0001301

Graham, S., Kiuhara, S. A., & MacKay, M. (2020). The effects of writing on learning in science, social studies, and mathematics: A meta-analysis. *Review of Educational Research*, 90(2), 179–226. https://doi.org/10.3102/0034654320914744

Gray, Peter, The value of play I: The definition gives us insights. *Psychology Today* November 19, 2008 https://www.psychologytoday.com/us/blog/freedom-learn/200811/the-value-play-i-the-definition-play-gives-insights

Lawson, Alyssa, Ayala, Brittany, & Son, Ji. (2021). Priming students to calculate inhibits sense-making. *Journal of Cognitive Science*, 22(1), 41–69.

Resources

Högberg, Björn, Lindgren, Joakim, Johansson, Klara, Mattias Strandh, & Solveig Petersen (2021). Consequences of school grading systems on adolescent health: evidence from a Swedish school reform. *Journal of Education Policy*, 36(1), 84–106. https://doi.org/10.1080/02680939.2019.1686540

Knight, M., & Cooper, R. (2019). Taking on a new grading system: The interconnected effects of standards-based grading on teaching, learning, assessment, and student behavior. *NASSP Bulletin*, 103(1), 65–92. https://doi.org/10.1177/0192636519826709

Kohn, Alfie *What Works Better Than Traditional Math Instruction, From Chapter 9: "Getting the 3 R's Right"in The Schools Our Children Deserve.* Boston: Houghton Mifflin, 1999. https://www.alfiekohn.org/article/works-better-traditional-math-instruction/

Skene, Kayleigh, O'Farrelly, Christine M., Byrne, Elizabeth M., Kirby, Natalie, Stevens, Eloise C., & Ramchandani, Paul G. (2022). Can guidance during play enhance children's learning and development in educational contexts? A systematic review and meta-analysis. *Child Development.* https://doi.org/10.1111/cdev.13730

University of Cambridge. Learning through 'guided' play can be as effective as adult-led instruction up to at least age eight: Play-based learning may also have a more positive effect on younger children's acquisition of important early maths skills compared with traditional, direct instruction. *ScienceDaily. ScienceDaily*, January 12, 2022. www.sciencedaily.com/releases/2022/01/220112094006.htm

2

The Town and Neighborhood

Towns and Neighborhoods: Philosophy and Application

The concept of towns and neighborhoods is common enough for children to have an understanding of what they are, while also presenting lots of opportunities for challenge and depth. Presented as a model for play and exploration, the themes surrounding "town" or "neighborhood" are vast in learning opportunities. Through experiential learning that takes place within various "Town Spaces", children are offered the opportunity to co-construct simulations of businesses and shops in order to:

- ♦ develop more concrete knowledge about abstract concepts
- ♦ help design and co-create more efficient play systems and simulations through active problem solving and troubleshooting
- ♦ use and gain experience with new vocabulary and materials

- ♦ share their insights regarding their observations and reflections of play within their class community
- ♦ engage and participate in open-ended projects that are fun, are relevant and which provide students with choice, agency, and new vehicles for learning.

These projects are all designed to provide students with enriching experiences that help them *make sense* of the world around them by giving them a chance to *play with* the ideas, vocabulary, and experience of working within a REAL shop or store. Teachers and students work in tandem to bring play to life in a back-and-forth dance of co-creation. Along the way, conversations are constantly taking place and observations are made and documented as the children become more and more engrossed in the work of play. Finally, students reflect on what they've "figured out" and observed about the system through writing, photographs, and collective observations and dialogue.

While some of the projects are simple, others will take several years of practice to fully grow to be in "full swing", so starting small and adding features from year to year is recommended. Keep in mind that none of these projects are intended to be "perfect"; rather, they aim to keep PLAY at the center of the experience and incorporate some of the tools and boundaries of the real world to help give shape and form towards developing an understanding.

Before moving on to reading about each of the various stores, theaters, and places that pop up in this imaginary town, first take some time to imagine your own classroom as a house within a neighborhood of classrooms that all together form a town. Children appreciate thinking of school in this way, as it immediately provides them with grounding as well as a sense of belonging. Within neighborhoods and towns, everyday people work at all different kinds of jobs, and different kinds of shops and businesses are important to the community. Students bring these various businesses and shops to life through imaginative play, cooperative work, and organizing and creating systems to solve problems.

The Bank

Overview
The Bank forms the foundation for many of the other projects in this chapter. As the shops listed later in this chapter begin to intertwine, the Bank becomes more and more integral in its role within the town and neighborhood. This project outline focuses on developing a banking center and culture within the classroom and can complement grade specific standards around money and exchange, fractions, place value, and/or counting and number sense.

Through playful and repeated practice, students learn that the Bank is a space to work on being accurate and fair when exchanging currencies. Later, as the Bank becomes a familiar center, students self-manage and operate individual accounts and the designated currency system. Once established as a core center, the Bank can "open" and "close" as needed as it forms an essential base for many of the other projects in "The Town Neighborhood".

Goals
The goal is for students to work in a class community bank and develop vocabulary and deepening conceptual understanding around banking and financial literacy. Specific goals for math include:

- working with and documenting equivalencies within various math manipulatives
- practicing making fair exchanges
- developing methods of organizing accounts
- improving accuracy in counting and record keeping.

Time Frame/Age Group
This is a good project to place at the beginning of the year, as it begins in a more exploratory and procedural way and then can be reintroduced throughout the year. Project time varies from a one-week set-up period to being used as needed throughout the year. It is appropriate for all ages of elementary students.

Materials
- An attractive area of the classroom to serve as a banking area – it's helpful to have a service counter or desk for tellers to serve customers
- Play telephones, calculators, other "tools" of an office and banking setting
- Various math manipulatives to serve as currency
- Pocket charts and containers that can hold individual account manipulatives or currencies
- Cash or money box
- Abacus, 10 frames or counting beads
- Working computer that students can use
- Accounting and balance sheets (You can use spreadsheets on the computer but to start, a large collective accounting sheet will work)

Preparation/Difficulty Level: Varies
The difficulty level varies in this project as the complexity of the banking system slowly builds from imaginative play into a more organized and independent system self-managed by the class community. This can be a very simple project or come to mirror complexity close to any real-life banking system.

Besides providing tools and setting up an attractive area in the classroom or school for the Bank to operate, it is most important to have a clear idea of the currencies you will be using to help children gain experience noticing and listing equivalencies and making exchanges. Take the time to review your math manipulatives along with your own goals and grade level standards and how you plan to use them to create a system of equal trades, depending on your particular curricular needs. For example, if you are working on decimals with students, are you planning on starting with Cuisenaire rods or coins? Below is a sample list of some manipulatives you may like to try and the grades that may best correspond to the tools:

- Counting bears (K-2)
- Unifix cubes (K-5)
- Pattern blocks (K-5)

- Base 10 blocks (2-5)
- Cuisenaire rods (2-5)
- Coins (K-5)
- Coins and bills (K-5)

Layout and Design

Recreating an entire banking system is a complex undertaking. Therefore, this project occurs in two distinct phases. The first phase is focused on moving students from simply playing with math manipulatives to seeing them as currency. This is done through a slow process that allows lots of time for play and exploration, inquiry, and finally, student documentation of their findings. This exploration time also helps establish community procedures, norms, and practices within the Bank as children negotiate their way through problems that naturally arise when conflict occurs during play.

Phase two of the project is the applications and operational phase, where the procedures and norms that have been initially established in the Bank are then used more operationally as they form a "center within a center" of other projects outlined in this chapter.

Phase One: Establishing General Banking Practices and Procedures

Setting Up for Open Play and Exploration

The first step to this project is opening the center. *It does not have to be fully complete before you open it!* In fact, it is better to let the center "evolve into being" as you slowly place objects and tools that catch the interest of the students, and they inform you what they need to bring it to life. They can "talk on the phone to potential customers" or "work the numbers" on calculators, beginning to imagine the Bank into being. For grades 2 and under, this will be a natural and seamless flow. For older grades, they may hesitate to jump in to play, so add more complex tools like accounting ledgers, spreadsheets, and organizational tasks designed to catch their attention and interest. Whether they jump right in or hold back, the mood of the center should be playful, open-ended, and unscripted as students and teachers work to co-create the area.

As you add materials to the center, children filter in and out as they are curious to explore the new area. At this stage, there is ebb and flow and you and the students work to co-create and explore the bank setup and area. The play is dynamic, unscripted, open-ended, and directed by the children.

For those unaccustomed to incorporating play into the academic setting, you may be thinking, "But I don't know what to DO." As facilitator, you set the stage, provide materials and structures, create the invitation, and then spend time observing how your students begin to use the space. It may take time and you may need to tweak a few things, but presented correctly within an open atmosphere where children feel safe enough to explore and play, eventually someone will pick up the ball. For older children, it may take a bit of doing, as they "play it cool" and they may need a more formal introduction and sense of permission to help them begin to settle into the idea of engaging in imaginative play within the classroom setting. Keep in mind that older children love to trade character cards, baseball cards and stickers, all which could be used as an integral part of this project.

Once play breaks through and begins to bloom, depending on your class, and most definitely for younger aged children, problems and conflicts may soon arise. Use those as opportunities for group reflection and problem solving. Talk openly about what you noticed, what they observed and work together to create workable solutions. Obviously, if the problem resides with one student, pull them over to discuss the issue in private. However, talking more generally and openly about conflicts during play is extremely important because it often leads to key insights about larger systemic and global issues and problems, such as:

- There aren't enough materials for everyone.
- There is only one job open, and many people want to work there.
- There is confusion about procedures.
- A system needs to be developed around conflict resolution.

Openly engaging in sharing and reflection is a key component in each of the Play Projects. The more students see how you value and honor their play, the freer they feel to express themselves. Write down students' insights to facilitate documentation and embed regular class discussions as part of following up play sessions and help foster connections between the issues and problems that arise within the classroom and those that are happening in the real world.

For currency, it is helpful to start with one specific manipulative. Whether it is counting bears, pattern blocks or Unifix cubes, students will want to work with the manipulatives in an open-ended and representational way. Tailor the manipulatives and structures depending on your specific mathematical goals. To help set up the Bank, students can:

- create groups of 10 and bundles of 100 using Unifix cubes
- place counters on a 10 frame
- explore Cuisenaire rods or pattern blocks
- organize and sort place value cubes
- use and organize coins and play money.

This should all be done with the spirit of open-ended discovery. Adding 10 frames or similar self-correcting structures and materials within the Banking center can provide students with the extra time and support they need to reinforce concepts and skills they may need more practice using.

Gaining Experience with Exchange and Fair Trades

Once there is a buzz in the air and the center has been "adopted" by the children, it's time to slowly add some structure. As children are working with the manipulatives, begin asking questions and making observations. For example, if you were using pattern blocks as a currency, ask, "If I were to trade you 3 green triangles for a yellow hexagon, would you consider that a fair trade?" The goal is to slowly move students from playing abstractly with the manipulatives to beginning to think about the tool as a mathematical equivalency that is important and relevant to the Bank.

After some exploration, begin to add some form of "official training" by casually mentioning one day if anyone would like to "work a job" as a teller, and note that there are applications and training sessions available. You can call this "training" or not, depending on your group and your style. Whatever playful form it takes, the idea is that as part of the play, students need to begin to demonstrate some type of skill to be qualified to work certain positions at the Bank.

Ask students to organize and document a logical and predictable system of fair exchange and equivalencies within whichever manipulatives you are using and to create lists and documentation of their findings. They can do this within a group or individually. You might be surprised that it will take them some time to both notice the patterns and occurrences and then to organize the list of fair exchanges in an orderly fashion. Don't tell them how to organize their discoveries, but rather keep up the inquiry by asking questions and making observations, allowing them time to figure it out themselves and providing opportunities for students to share their work and findings with the class.

Keep discussions flowing and open as students discover concepts by working with a specific set of manipulatives and making observations about their equivalencies. As you've tailored the particular manipulative to your curricular needs, the challenge and relevancy to your program are already embedded within the work. When students have stuck with it for a while and produced a list, that can serve as their official qualification as a Banker. They can then incorporate their documentation as part of their math portfolio.

The next stage is finding equivalencies using a second type of currency. For some grades, this is where you might introduce play money into the center, or conversely, remove the money and introduce Cuisenaire rods, all depending on your math goals. The students again explore, discover, list, and organize the equivalencies they notice. For those needing an added challenge, they can work to see if there might be systems of equivalencies between two different "currencies" or manipulatives. Adding digital tools here will yield even more possibilities for exploration, as many digital tools give students more concrete ways of making connections between mathematical concepts. Make sure students record and document their findings to add to their math portfolios, which are discussed more in depth in Chapter Five. Once students have completed introductory procedures and practices, the first phase of the Banking systems project is complete, and it can be "closed" until needed for the next project.

Phase Two: Operational Community Banking
Operational Integration
Once willing students have demonstrated knowledge of making fair trades and finding equivalencies, they have gained the basic job skills needed to work at the Bank.
Phase two of the Bank is focused on:

a. the opening of individual bank accounts
b. the resulting need for methods of earning and reasons to trade currencies.

a. Individual accounts and accounting
   Accounts open up a whole new avenue of exploration and complexity. To start small, have students begin to open individual accounts with a seed fund provided by you, the "government", and just play with the idea of making deposits and withdrawals within the Bank setting. To further the idea of accounts, students can be charged processing fees and/or receive interest payments.

   Inevitably, credit cards will come up. Document students' questions and encourage their exploration and reading on this angle. See what kinds of systems of accounting they can come up with themselves and what problems they encounter when testing their systems in the play scenarios. Perhaps a credit card company pops up or the Bank decides to start making loans to customers in good standing. Some procedures that may be established or explored at this point in the play could be:
   - the need for work shifts and schedules
   - opening procedures to establish individual bank accounts

- procedures and forms for making withdrawals and deposits
- fair rates of exchange
- accounting practices.

b. Methods of earning and reasons to trade

Now that students have an account, what will they do with their money? Some students may decide to just keep it in the Bank, where it can earn an x% rate of interest. Others may decide they want to make more money and so want to go "across the street" within the classroom to where a brand-new investment firm has suddenly popped up. The investment firm advertisement says it is giving a y% rate of return, but they might lose some of their money if the rate changes. Students can decide what they would like to do. Highly qualified Bankers may decide to work at the investment firm or start another one in a different area of the classroom. Some things that may be established through problem solving and play at this point include:

- how money is being earned or distributed among students
- procedures for accurate exchange and accounting
- how interest rates are calculated and distributed for Banking savings accounts or investments
- the problem of physical storage of amounts of money
- establishment of additional investment firms or alternate investment opportunities including a stock market
- how investment firms and the Bank raise money and earn capital without government loans
- what happens when Banks and investment firms run out of money.

Integrations

The Bank becomes an important system for the "Neighborhood Town" once money comes into play and systems of commerce begin to develop, as outlined later in this chapter in the Grocery Store and Money Town projects. Refer to those projects to see how the Bank works within those projects.

Outcomes and assessments

By the end of Phase One of this project, students should have documented evidence of equivalencies of at least two different math manipulatives that they have listed, drawn, photographed, or shown using digital manipulatives. Students should be able to show evidence of all the possible combinations when using pattern blocks, for example. Decide how much evidence students should provide according to your individual needs and make sure to incorporate the documentation as part of individual student math portfolios.

By the end of Phase Two, students should know that the Bank is a place that:

- handles the flow of money
- provides fair and equitable exchange
- is central to the development of economies
- must maintain accurate accounting practices
- provides a safe space for the community to keep their money
- may charge fees and/or offer interest payments on accounts
- may provide loans to qualified student borrowers.

Older students can write out their observations and insights of how the Bank system works and what problems they faced and solved. Collect quotes from both younger and older students throughout the project to serve as documentation of the collective learning that has occurred. This can all be presented together with the evidence of ability to make fair trades, as recorded in their individual portfolio.

Troubleshooting

The danger here is for adults to become too regimented or eager for children to discover the fair trades and equivalencies within math manipulatives in Phase One, so that they end up doing the "discovering" for the students through "instruction", rather than allowing enough time and space for students to explore the materials enough to make the discovery on their own. If students are taking an exceedingly long time or using the manipulatives in ways that counteract the project (i.e., building houses with them, etc.) you may want to change out that manipulative from the Banking center and try another to help them make the connection more easily. This is where working between digital manipulatives and the physical tools can also be of great help.

Phase two of the project requires some finesse as a playful and creative exchange is needed rather than a rigid, instructional approach. You may be very surprised to see what problems naturally arise through play, how relevant they are to the real world of banking, and how children can understand that firsthand when given the opportunity to play within a system.

The Bank has been established as a place of fair and equitable exchange and can now open and close as needed. It is a fluid system that can be reopened when needed by other community projects, namely, Money Town, outlined later in this chapter and the Grocery Store, outlined next.

The Grocery Store

Overview
The Grocery Store is a wonderful example of the power of experiential learning for elementary-school-aged children and shows how cross-curricular integrations and applications can work together within one project. While this project is layered and takes time to build to full capacity, even when done on a small scale, it helps students build a deep understanding of economics along with math and literacy skills and concepts.

Goals
The overall goal of this project is that students will build a basic understanding of economic systems through working in a simulated grocery store. Specific academic goals will fluctuate depending on the grade level of the student. Some may include:

- ♦ K-5 Food systems, scarcity, and issues of economic and social justice

- K-2 Working with environmental print, sorting, and categorizing items, and developing and applying mathematical fact fluency
- 3-5 Developing sensemaking around economic systems and real-world mathematical skill application.

Time Frame/Age Group

This two-to-three-week project works well with all elementary grade students, whether in individual classes or as a larger collective community project.

Materials
- An area to serve as the Grocery Store center
- Food (can be plastic play food as is often found in Early Childhood programs or, preferably, actual cans of food that are collected from the community to be later donated to food pantries)
- Cash registers
- Counter area for cashiers to work
- Shelving areas to sort and store food
- 2 sets of alphabet cards (1 for shelves and the other for a pricing list)
- Child-sized school chairs that can easily scoot along on the flooring (to serve as grocery carts)
- Baskets
- Brooms and dustpans
- Grocery bags
- Scales for weighing items
- Lanyards or name tag badges with clearly marked job titles (This also helps put limits on the amount of people who can be working at the same time)
- Timecards (to track work shifts)
- Child-sized aprons for stockers and grocery workers
- Large paper for visible pricing lists
- Forms to serve as receipts for cashiers and shoppers
- Music (preferably "elevator type" music, appropriate to a grocery store setting)
- Area to serve as the Bank (refer back to the Bank project to see materials needed)

Preparation/Difficulty Level: Medium
This project is fairly easy to set up; what makes it complex is how expansive it can become. As with each project listed in this book, start small and incorporate new features as you gain experience.

Layout and Design
The first thing to decide about this project is your sourcing and plan for the food in the Grocery Store. Are you going to use pretend plastic food or are you going to have students bring donations in from home as part of a school Food and Supplies Drive to donate to a local food pantry or organization? While plastic food may have fewer complications, it is also a less environmentally-friendly and community-friendly option – but an option, nonetheless.

There are many benefits to using donated goods, but before doing so, it is important that the children are not looking at them as a "toy" or as a "prop". While you may need to remove some breakable items from the Grocery Store, children are perfectly capable of being careful stewards of a community's generous donations, especially when they are given the chance to show they can do so.

> *It is essential to the integrity of the project that all donations and items are handled by the students with reverence and respect.*

Having regular conversations surrounding food scarcity is core to the project and helps inform essential knowledge around topics of social and economic justice for students to regularly discuss, think about and write about as part of the project. Through the experience of working with the groceries, the items become beloved and take on new meaning; when it is time to give them away, students have developed a deeper and more authentic appreciation of the importance and impact of their donation.

Some of the kinds of questions to visit and revisit frequently surrounding this topic might be:

- ♦ What kinds of things do people need to live?
- ♦ Where do people get food?

- Does food grow at the grocery store? If not, where does it come from?
- How do people get money?
- What other things besides food do people need to live well and be healthy?
- What happens if there are no grocery stores or if grocery stores are far away from where people live?
- What do people do if they can't walk or drive to the store?
- Do grocery stores help people? If so, how?
- How do cold places get fresh food in winter?
- What do people do when food for their family costs 10 units, but their job only pays 5 units?
- What can people do to help each other get food?
- How should you take care of something you are giving to someone?

After some conversation, next comes the design and layout of the actual grocery store and commerce system. You will need a checkout area for shoppers and empty shelving for the Grocery Store, as well as a Banking area to facilitate the exchange of currency.

Shopping area:
- Open shelving with room to sort items alphabetically
  One set of alphabet cards is used to designate where food is shelved and the other is used to list prices. Sorting alphabetically provides younger students experience with reading environmental print as they can decide if a can of "peas" is to be shelved in the "P" section or the "V" for "vegetables" section. Prices are sorted alphabetically as well, so as to avoid having to price every single item. For example, anything that starts with the letter "P" costs "5", while items starting with "T" might cost "7" or whatever unit you decide upon.
- Grocery carts
  School chairs work really well as grocery carts as they can glide on school flooring quietly. Add a basket to the seat of the chair and voilà – you have a grocery cart!

Checkout counter:
- Checkout counters should be stocked with cash registers, pricing lists, receipts and bags or baskets.
- As mentioned previously, prices correspond with the alphabet. Decide your prices depending on the type of calculations you are looking to reinforce. Using whole numbers makes the project more accessible for all elementary ages, while you may want to use prices containing decimals for older ages of students.
- While anything in the store that begins with the letter "M" may cost "8", you can adjust the difficulty by introducing 10%-off coupons for older children or special pricing, for example "½ off", for younger students. Pricing can also depend on the type of currency you decide to use, whether it be Unifix cubes or play money, as that may change the flexibility you have with pricing items.
- Deciding your currency and pricing can take a while and should be thought through carefully by the teacher.

Banking area:
- As students will be "paying" for their groceries, they will need a place to store and keep their money as well as make currency trades when needed. The Bank holds all the money and accounts, which can be a physical accounting method or done through a spreadsheet, however you and the Bank staff decide.
- This will become a busy area as students will be making deposits and withdrawals as they secure jobs and go shopping, so plan accordingly. Refer to the previous project that outlines the Bank area for more details about setup needs.
- Guidance for using Unifix cubes as "currency":
  - Unifix cubes are a good basic alternative currency for multi-aged groups.
  - Bankers build "towers of 10" by color and do a complete inventory of the total "money" available.
  - Bankers can give each shopper a seed amount of 5 or 10 as an introduction to the system until shoppers earn their own money.

- A pocket chart can serve as a home for "debit cards" should you choose to introduce them as the project progresses.

Staffing and Jobs:
- Students operate the whole system, stockers, to cashiers, managers, and bankers. They "earn" money/currency by working at various jobs that earn various amounts of money.
- Job descriptions:
  - Bankers organize and count the initial amount of money in the Bank. Give each Shopper "10", or whatever amount is chosen as seed to start. They issue and keep track of individual student accounts. Decide how much Bankers earn depending on your needs and in proportion to grocery prices.
  - Stockers keep the shelves stocked with new and returning inventory. (Once Shoppers "buy" the groceries, Stockers carefully return the grocery items to the stock area and the play sequence repeats.) Stockers make decisions like, "Do mashed potatoes go in the "M" aisle or the "P" aisle?" Stocking is a great job for kindergarten through second graders. When not busy, they can track and maintain accounting for inventory, organize shelves and help keep the store clean. Decide how much they earn and either keep track of their working shift or ask them to report to another student acting as a stocker manager.
  - Cashiers check out the shoppers with accurate accounting practices, provide receipts and bag groceries. Cashier pay is to be decided along with the other jobs and roles.
  - Shoppers buy groceries and use the Bank. Keep it playful, but should they need a push towards pretend play, inspire by inviting them to plan dinners and make lists of what they need to "purchase".

Scaffolding

As with every project, start small and slowly add elements as you gain experience and confidence. To begin, children enjoy the imaginative, playful roles of "shopping", checking out and returning items to be stocked. It is important to give the project "time to bloom" as students help create and set up the area and drive the excitement with their imaginative play within the center. You may want to have a "limit of 5 items" depending on the stock available and before they start loading their carts up and emptying the shelves.

After there is a playful flow, the system will naturally start needing support and maintenance. Layer in jobs and roles to support the system as necessary. Children will naturally fill and find many of the roles and jobs as you create new ones together. Supply workers with tools and materials like aprons and name tags to help designate their roles as workers.

Gradually add structure by introducing pricing. Pricing can exist for some time without introducing actual currencies, as students are happy to pretend to "pay 5" while being a Cashier or Shopper. This gives you time to get the Bank set up and running. Bankers work to organize currency. To introduce currency, gradually ask Bankers to start giving shoppers "10" or whatever amount you have decided to start with, while then working with Cashiers to start charging actual currency for goods. Cashiers can begin to complete itemized receipts to help them keep track of the customers' purchases and help them keep track of adding multiple items. If tuna fish comes in a pack of six and each "T" costs "4", how much does the customer need to pay? Would they get a better deal if they were charged under "F" for "fish" at "3" per can? Does the customer have a coupon for "½ off"? Or perhaps there is a 20%-off sale on items L-Z? Cashiers have big jobs, and it can be great practice for fact fluency when calculating items.

Once pricing and currency is introduced and you've flooded the market with some start-up cash, things will really start humming. Shoppers will blow through that initial cash quickly, so they will need to work a job to earn money. They should be paid per shift to help reinforce that work equals money. It can be a paper paycheck that the bankers then redeem, or a physical currency, depending on your system's needs and constraints. Hiring a "Manager" may be a good idea at this point to help keep track of all the workers' shifts. Are they short on Cashiers? Up their pay. Do they have too many Stockers? Limit their working hours. The Manager should help decide these policies and changes. It's amazing how remarkably easy and yet difficult it is at the same time to recreate an entire economic system.

Integrations
One of the primary reasons for this project is to help **students** recognize the impact of economics in our everyday lives, in terms of both the realities and the inequities. When the project finds itself in dire need of Bankers, the pay for Bankers goes up from 7 to 10 units. Children immediately understand supply and demand, and the value and importance of fair wages and labor. When the Stockers fall short on the job and the shelves are empty, Shoppers notice. Cashiers may feel like they are working harder than the Bankers but receiving less pay. Through regular group discussions, these topics come up and are noticed and valued as part of both assessment and active student learning.

Challenges surrounding the proportion of a worker's pay to food costs provide students with a deep understanding of the difficulties many families face in securing regular meals, even when working hard at full time jobs. This, in turn, helps build understanding around the importance of community giving and support systems.

Other ways of integrating academic subjects into the store are:

- the art of ads and advertisements
- multiple languages through food labels
- global education through exposure to different varieties and types of food donations
- food nutrition labels
- inventory counts
- labels and job descriptions.

Outcomes and Assessments

The purpose of the Grocery Store is to give children an opportunity to engage in imaginative play and mathematical practice within a simulated economic system and then to make observations and share insights about the project. They can do this through individual written work or through group conversations and documented observations. Here are some observations made by a group of fourth graders who worked at the store during their social studies class time:

> *"You don't want to sell the food for too much because no one will want to buy it. Ten units is too much."*
>
> Stocker

> *"Some people have been shocked at the prices and have to change what they buy."*
>
> Cashier

> *"The Bank is important because it's the main route. You don't just get free money here; you have to work."*
>
> Banker

> *"Some people are overcharging – embezzling means overcharging, so the government might criticize the store and shut it down."*
>
> Stocker

> *"The workers take charge of their jobs. Sometimes there's arguments, but they find a way to work together."*
>
> Stocker

> *"Speaking as a manager, we have to check the receipts and check the Cashiers to make sure they aren't forgetting to mark down everything customers buy."*
>
> Manager

> *"We technically just had a problem with economics. There was a problem with receipts and Cashiers. The receipts didn't match*

the cash in the box, so we had to fix that by telling the Cashiers to be careful, otherwise they might get fired."

Manager

"In this job, it seems like our paychecks are going down. We don't have any customers right now because everyone is working. Maybe everyone should work for a limited time."

Stocker

"When people stop shopping, everything stops. The Bank stops working, the Bakery stops, the Cashiers stop, everything stops."

Cashier

What economic concepts do you think these quotes touch on? Would they have the same level of understanding and questions if they were to be copying vocabulary down from a textbook? Or working to create the system themselves, without the opportunity to play and live it? Regular group conversations should pepper the project consistently, with student wonderings, issues, and problems discussed, as they are central to the project. Document and revisit their questions and observations over and over again.

Additionally, the issue of food systems and social and economic justice and equity provides key content for students to investigate and reflect upon. Challenge them to feed a family of four on "10 units", vary the pay for Stockers and Cashiers to help drive home the fact that some jobs are hard work, but may pay less than others. Ask students why they think that is and to share their insights. Constant back and forth conversations about the play system intertwine to form both learning and assessment.

Students should write and reflect upon their experiences within the store to serve as documentation as a final assessment of the project. Be transparent about the aspects you are looking for students to discuss within their final written piece.

Troubleshooting

The number of issues that can come up in this project are infinite and will require flexibility, quick thinking, and open dialogue among students, teachers and the community. Being transparent about issues is a good policy, as students have incredible solutions and insights.

Beyond logistical issues is, again, the issue of adults becoming too rigid with the project and not allowing the children to take the reins of play. *It's better not to introduce any currency into the mix than it is to kill the project by making the Cashier job a chore.* The primary goal of the project is not computational practice, but rather to promote student sensemaking about economic concepts.

Extensions

Once the store is bustling and running smoothly, think about adding a Bakery, Cafe or incorporating fresh vegetables from the school garden. Incorporating cooking, recipes, and food and nutrition labels are natural extensions. In some school settings, conditions permitting, the Grocery Store could serve as a community Food Bank within itself. The possibilities for the Store are numerous as it involves so many key aspects of life within the community.

Resources

Tadayon, Ali, *EdSource*, March 30, 2020 https://edsource.org/2020/california-food-banks-partner-with-schools-to-serve-families-of-students/627322

Teaching Tolerance. *Beyond the Canned Food Drive*, Issue 32, Fall, 2007 https://www.learningforjustice.org/magazine/fall-2007/beyond-the-canned-food-drive

Museums, Kitchens, and Cafes

These next business model "pop-up projects" are less "projects" than they are cooperative play scenarios designed to present and showcase student work. The Cafe and Kitchens project model works well for students to cooperatively create and develop efficient systems while practicing a variety of language skills and improving self-regulation. The Museum model simply provides a framework for students to present their work to visitors. These project models can incorporate math, social studies (economics), literacy, and world languages/global education.

Overview
Student-operated businesses and systems showcase student work, providing a method for a final presentation for a project. Each of the "businesses" can also stand alone as a systems analysis project, where students help co-construct the system and reflect on the experience through written work and ongoing group discussion. This project also supports skill building surrounding executive functioning.

Goals
The goal is for students to operate a business or organization that provides a "Museum" tour experience and/or food or beverage service through the "Kitchens and Cafe" model for guests, as a culminating project event. Students will be able to explain verbally or through a written "How-To" piece regarding the organizational and cooperative systems needed in order to run a successful Cafe and Kitchen operation.

Time Frame/Age Group
This is a "plug-in" project that can operate for a few days, or as a one-time event if done as a celebration. As a full stand-alone project, it should run anywhere from two to three weeks. It is appropriate for all ages of elementary students.

Materials
For the Museum
Museum materials are a showcase of student work. If finishing up an Author Study, for example, individual student work related to the Study is presented through a museum tour model where students discuss and present the work to visitors. You will need an area suitable for a gallery where visitors can interact with the students' work. Students act as docents and host visitors or give tours of their individual piece or the whole body of

work, be it a completed art piece, piece of written work, poster, or invention.

For Kitchen and Cafe
- Cash register
- TV tray tables
- Small cups* (espresso, tea, or disposable cups)
- Small plates if serving food
- Small notepads for taking orders
- Napkins
- Menus (can be physical or memorized by servers, depending on your setup)
- Aprons or name tags to distinguish working roles (chef, server, host, docent)
- Beverage of choice: water, lemonade, tea, etc.
- Optional foods (Something can be cooked ahead of time or it can be as simple as a cookie or cracker)
- Music (as needed for atmosphere)

*If you can, use real glass espresso cups or small tea sets, as it adds an aura of realness to the setup and children genuinely appreciate and respect being entrusted with something breakable.

Preparation/Difficulty Level: Easy
This is a great project for anyone starting out managing large-scale, student-run, playful operations. Most every child knows something about how a restaurant, cafe, or kitchen works. You may be surprised at how easy it is for children to slip into the role of a server or chef or how excited older elementary students are at the opportunity to playfully create this type of business.

For the Kitchen and Cafe component, students gain experience by completing a series of training tasks before they work the job. Students practice walking around the classroom carrying trays with cups of water and working to fill orders. You can do this with other students acting as customers and taking turns becoming servers and chefs. Scaffold the practice sessions as necessary, depending on the age and ability of your students. Note how and when students are able to work smoothly when serving in a busy restaurant, as it highlights self-regulation and executive functioning skills in students. For those who may be struggling with executive functioning skills, provide extra time and practice carrying trays and cups of water through the maze and bustle of the classroom.

Layout and Design
The setting is important as you will need an area to serve as a "Kitchen" (even if you are just serving water or lemonade). For the Cafe area, make sure there is an attractive area for guests to sit comfortably at Cafe tables. It is helpful to practice several times as students help create routines and structures around making the system operate smoothly.

If a museum component is planned to showcase student work, decide whether it is a stand-alone Museum or whether it will have a Cafe as part of the experience. Museum Cafes can be separate areas connected to the Museum, or mobile units where students casually offer visitors a snack or beverage on trays.

Scaffolding
Training
Students practice carrying trays with cups and water to gain experience for the job. You can vary the difficulty and break it down into more specific steps to help students succeed and be challenged based on their age and grade. Once they are comfortable and feel skilled enough, they can progress to "chef" with as simple a job as pouring cups of water. Increase and vary the difficulty from there as desired.

Setup
The primary challenge in getting the system set up is organizing "student work shifts" so that not everyone is on the floor at the same time. If you are using a Cafe and Museum system together, it's easy to rotate the Museum docents and Cafe workers. Students can also read to guests while others serve and take orders. Whatever system you decide upon, having specific and clear amounts of time and shift designations is important as students are eager to work and be a part of the action of the Cafe.

To set up a museum, make sure there is a clear definition of where the exhibit begins and ends and be sure to include an explanation of the project threaded throughout. Treat student work as you would any curated exhibit, making sure it is attractive and able to "stand alone" in explaining the process of the work to visitors. When the Museum is "hosted" by student docents, they are there to provide visitors with details and information about the project and work. Be sure that students include relevant books, media, and materials to enhance the exhibit. Students can take charge of this process by working in groups to develop specific areas of the Museum.

Billing

For the Cafe, decide whether you are charging real money and if so, where the money will go, so that guests are prepared and informed. Donating the money to a cause or operating the Cafe to raise money for specific funds can be a unique and fun way for school community members to see students at work and play. Make sure that counting the money is done by students as part of the project. Alternatively, you can use a more generic "units" exchange using math manipulatives as currency. Whatever method you choose, make sure students provide guests with a bill and there is a system in place to handle payments. If you are just starting out, try operating the Cafe without money and work to incorporate the money component the next time.

Integrations

Once you and your students gain skill and experience in setting up Kitchens, Cafes, and Museums, they can come together easily and be used at any time. Some ideas to further integrate into the curriculum are:

- Host a "World Language Cafe" where students order using a designated second language.
- Use coins to make change, keep accurate accounting records and/or estimate costs and expenses.
- Incorporate math through varying the difficulty of cooking and measurement activities.

- Use foods from the community school garden to highlight the garden or local cooperative farm.
- Incorporate poetry, literary readings, or artwork into the Cafe.
- Museums can take on many forms, showcasing student inventions, artwork, or live demonstrations.

Outcomes and Assessments

Museum presentations are essentially an efficient way to manage student presentations, so instead of a one-by-one approach, they are done in a group rotational system or all at once. This can be a great time saver if you are short on time, yet still want to ensure students have time to publicly present their work. Assessing student work can be done by observing the thoroughness of their work and their individual presentations, and by having visitors provide helpful feedback to students through written guided prompts.

Assessing student work in the Cafe system yields interesting and informative observations for any educator, as it reveals itself to be a remarkable indicator of self-regulation and executive functioning skills. Students solve problems on the fly and scaffold tasks in an efficient way, all while serving customers and working spontaneously and collaboratively with their peers. Additionally, have students reflect on the system of the Kitchen and Cafe to see what they noticed in terms of what worked and what could be improved. Students can provide "How-To" writing and drawing samples to show how the Kitchen and Cafe system worked and complete written and visual descriptions of their observations and reflections of the project and system operations to serve as their final assessment piece.

Troubleshooting

If you are using real cups in the Cafe, washing and having enough dishes for guests can be tricky. Incorporating a dishwashing station can help but it comes with its own set of challenges, as it's hard to ensure dishes are sufficiently clean when students are in charge of dishwashing. Take the time to build a large collection of real cups slowly and over the course of years while slowly weaning off one-time-use paper cups and products.

The other area of trouble is ensuring there are fair work shifts and role divisions. Spend lots of time discussing how shifts are created and troubleshooting and creating fair systems where everyone who wants a turn to work can do so.

Extensions
- Combine with efforts within the Community Garden Project (as outlined in Chapter Four).
- Students can host a Cafe event as part of a night where parents, caregivers, and community members are invited to view student work within a museum model.
- Add more computational math practice by having students account for expenses as well as analyze profits either using general units or actual currency.

Stoplight Story Theater

Overview
Children's literature and written work comes to life within a theater of the pretend "Town and Neighborhood" concept. Poems and stories are told and reenacted by students through various types of performance theater.

Goals
Students interpret literature, write scripts, and perform short pieces for audiences. Primary literacy goals are fostering reading comprehension through scriptwriting, re-readings, and retellings, by having students break down literature into performance chunks. Other goals include working peers and fostering self-regulation through cooperative problem solving.

Time Frame/Age Group
This can be anywhere from a one-week to four-week project and is appropriate for all ages of elementary grade levels.

Materials
- Books and literature approachable and challenging enough to be interpreted by students within a reasonable amount of time
- Stage area with seating
- Supporting set design and costumes, as appropriate or available
- Scriptwriting materials
- Tickets (can be made/photocopied)
- Programs (add student biographies should you have time)

Preparation/Difficulty Level: Medium
This is a fairly easy project to put together. However, what can make it difficult is the social DRAMA that tends to come along with any theater project. Fair warning: it can be intense, but with proper management, bringing stories to life through the theater is a rewarding and relatively easy project that makes a big splash into any curriculum and helps students develop and further their relationship with literature, while furthering writing and reading comprehension skills.

Layout and Design
What makes Stoplight Story Theater different from other performance types of projects is that it is focused more on the playful practice and creation of performing than it is focused on an actual performance. It's playing more with the idea of the theater than it is worried or concerned about putting on a perfect show. Frequent, low-stakes performances provide lots of time for creativity, drama and expression without the pressures and demands of a formal show.

Poetry readings, musicals, storytelling, puppetry, interpretive dance, and straight-up retellings and adaptations are all on the menu. The variations on this theme are as diverse as the offerings in any real theater. If you need inspiration, look to your local theater or any robust theater to see the breadth of their programming. As with each project in this book, start small and with the familiar, practice, and then branch out to the next stage.

While many schools and classrooms are familiar with Reader's Theater, the Stoplight Story Theater is where students playfully do the work of writing the dialogue, staging the play, deciding the parts, and putting on the final show.

You may want to begin this project with students selecting a piece of poetry to memorize or write and present. This can become an initial piece that they can always refer to or use as a "commercial break" during any show. For the next show, you may want to move on to small groups of students presenting a short piece of literature to foster reading comprehension. Picture books work exceptionally well here and come in all "reading levels" to ensure all levels of readers can be challenged. Bringing a wordless picture book to life might be even more challenging. Students should work to rewrite the piece into a formal script. The scriptwriting is what makes it a "Stoplight Story" in that the story is written out piece by piece and retold through the model of a traffic light:

- ♦ Green light: Actors first announce the show, the author of their piece and their names and specific roles and parts. The story begins. Action!
- ♦ Yellow light: The story is retold carefully, step by step, and slowly enough for the audience to understand what is happening. Do they have all the parts of the story? Does the story make sense? Is it being represented in a logical sequence? The "yellow light" helps students "slow down" and not miss critical parts of the story.
- ♦ Red light: This is the most abstract part of the theater experience which asks the actors to discuss and share, "What was this story about?" This can be embedded within the storytelling, done at the end in a presentation format or as a "salon" where the actors sit and discuss the piece with the audience after the performance. Whatever format you decide upon, the goal is for the students to be able to offer their reflections, inferences, thoughts, and interpretations of the piece of literature. Can you answer what the story "The Three Little Pigs" is about?

Scaffolding
Beginning:
- Decide on the book, show, and groups.
- Students read the book and talk to each other about possible plans.
- "Green light" practice and performance sessions

Middle:
- Troubleshooting practice sessions
- "Yellow light" practice and performance sessions
- Scriptwriting session
- "Red light" practice and performance sessions
- Troubleshooting practice sessions

End:
- Design sets, costumes, and tickets.
- Final performances

You can also approach this project a number of different structural ways depending on your needs:

- Small groups all do the same book and discuss the variety of ways in which it was staged (a good way to start the project).
- Small groups each do a book within a topic or author's collection.
- One large class takes on one book as a cast ensemble.
- Two groups compare/contrast pieces of literature.
- Students create their own versions of familiar tales.

Whatever structure you decide upon, if you are creating small group presentations, it is helpful to do several "low stake" practice sessions where groups have lots of time to work together and you have the opportunity to see how cooperatively they work with one another.

Integrations
A good way to introduce the project is by having students memorize or present a poem. From there they can move on to writing

commercials (great for opinion piece writing). Incorporate technology by videoing the commercials and having them edit the videos, if age appropriate. Weave the poems and commercial breaks into the breaks between the final skits and plays.

Outcomes and Assessments

Between the scriptwriting, final performances, and all the effort students put in to create simple set design, all while working cooperatively, there are plentiful opportunities for assessment within this project. Depending on your age group, review with students your expectations of the quality and details in retelling and scriptwriting you are looking for as a reflection of their learning. To support this, it's helpful to have several practice performance sessions where their peers can offer feedback. This also provides a nice segue into discussions with students about constructive criticism. Guide your students throughout the process to help ensure their success.

Troubleshooting

While it may be tempting to break up a chapter, book or piece of literature and have different groups of students each take a part, doing so may cause some confusion for some children in regard to supporting their comprehension. In that case, consider using puppets to keep the "actors" the same to help ensure continuity between characters.

The use of puppets can also be a great vehicle to help support students who may be shy when it comes to acting, as it gives them a bit of separation between themselves and the audience. Be aware that using puppets can get a bit silly until students have had enough time to settle in and become more accustomed to using them for storytelling.

Extensions

- Take your show "on the road" and do pop-up performances throughout the school.
- Incorporate music, art, and world languages into the performances through set design, inventing musical numbers and enhancing and diversifying dialogue.

- Film the performances and have students edit the final piece.
- Incorporate technology through set design or by presenting works through animation or with digital storytelling.

Resources and References
Reader's Theatre https://readerstheater.com/

Toy Town Makerspace

Overview
Toy Town is an engineering, design, and literacy project where students invent models for new toys.

Goals
The goal is for students to use elements of design and engineering to create and invent a toy for mass reproduction that includes "How-To" instructional writing.

Time Frame/Age Group:
This is a 3-to-4-week project, appropriate for all ages.

Materials
The list of materials in a Makerspace is extensive. While you can move into using more complex engineering materials, consider starting simply with less expensive and readily available materials so as to not become fully consumed with and caught up in the design process, and forgetting the documentation for mass reproduction angle of the project. Vary the material limits of the project depending on how much time/money/space you have. Some materials you may want to provide students with access to are:

- a large selection and options of craft and office supplies
- cardboard, tape, scissors, glue, and recycled materials
- paper and pencils for students to draw and write.

In the later stages of the project, you may consider adding more expensive engineering and building materials such as:

- "design and build" construction toys that include various sizes of wheels, tinker toys, Lego bricks, K'NEX, ETI Toys, Toy Pal construction toys, etc.
- circuit boards, batteries, LED lights
- computers to power or operate digitally operated toys.

Preparation/Difficulty Level: Medium

This is a project that requires a moderate amount of preparation and management, depending on the materials you are using. Setup and management largely consists of presenting and organizing the materials in a way that students can access them, assisting in the design process as needed, and ensuring they complete the directions and drawings for each of their designs.

Layout and Design

Many schools have implemented some form of a Makerspace into their school footprint. However, integrating these spaces into a curriculum can often be a challenge for schools and teachers, especially when it comes to elementary-aged students. "Toy Town" embeds literacy skills directly into the design work of inventing toys, as students are challenged to draw and write the directions of "how to" construct their toy for mass assembly by their peers or younger or older schoolmates. For this reason, it is helpful to start with readily available and low-cost materials.

Any place in the school setting or classroom area can be transformed into "Toy Town". When looking for a space, it's helpful for many elementary school teachers to begin thinking of it as a "Construction Zone" or "Arts and Crafts" area vs. a "Makerspace", as that can freeze up many teachers who may not be sure footed around technology. Every Early Childhood teacher is familiar and comfortable with construction zones and arts and crafts centers, as they form essential areas within the Early Years classroom. Look to Early Years educators to serve as leaders to help set up "Makerspace" areas within older elementary classroom areas or within a common area of the school.

Once you have assembled a wide variety of materials, students are then challenged to create and design a toy for mass reproduction. Students will need time to explore the materials and face their design challenges, working to refine their inventions. Encourage students to stop and share their thinking frequently. Once they have reached a satisfactory design, students draw and write out the steps for reproduction.

Scaffolding

Modify the writing structures for the various grades within the elementary school setting. For example, young students can fill out a basic form by drawing sequenced steps (1, 2, 3, 4) of how they made their toy and provide written labels for the drawings. First and second grade students can complete a similar form with more sequenced steps, including labels and written instructions, while third, fourth and fifth graders can complete more detailed instructional narratives along with sequenced drawings and labels.

Integrations

Literacy is thoroughly embedded into this unit as it accomplishes many of the goals of nonfiction writing through this engineering craft and design project. Integrate math by having older elementary students calculate the expense and cost of making each toy.

Outcomes and Assessments

Collections of each of the students' designs can be combined to form a "Toy Town" instruction manual made by the entire community, along with each of the physical toy designs displayed alongside their written work in a "Toy Town Workshop Showcase" for the school community to view. Students can also gain leadership and speaking experience by pitching and presenting their top final designs to classmates, guests, and the school community.

Assessment can be based on their written work and final design or a rubric you construct with your students to help them identify what makes a successful toy design. Incorporate the students' own expectations and requirements for what they would consider to be successful toy designs.

Troubleshooting

Managing multiple design projects and written instructions can be tricky. Having students work in pairs may help reduce the number of projects to manage. You can also buy some time by having students who are further along in the design process go through "peer review" groups who can help troubleshoot or offer constructive feedback about their models.

One of the most basic issues may be supplies, as they can be costly. This project would work with very basic supplies as well. Children can invent a lot with paper, paper clips, cardboard, tape, tin foil, and pipe cleaners. Many children will also need to complete their full design before writing and drawing the instructions; just be sure they complete the written portion of the project to ensure their toy can be reproduced.

Extensions

Some ideas for extending the project include:

- Add pricing costs.
- Group testing of recreating toy designs (Does the assembly line work based on the students' written instructions?).
- Design approvals and critiques by "toy testers".
- Vary the design constraints.
- Have students create marketing plans and packages.
- Students create commercials for their toys.
- Pitch the plan to a real toy maker company.

Resources

For in depth reading, resources and references regarding makerspaces and engineering in the classroom:

1	2
3	4

FIGURE 2.1
Sample showing basic blank form for an Early Years "How-To" sequence drawing.

Gary Stager, Ph.D has created mini kits for Makerspace projects on his blog, http://stager.tv/?p=5651 and has more extensive resource lists and projects related to making and constructing. His website https://inventtolearn.com/ and book *Invent to Learn* contain numerous resources and are essential reference guides for those more curious about using Makerspaces and engineering in the classroom. Another book you may want to reference is *Making in the K-3 Classroom: Why, How and Wow!* by Alice Baggett.

Money Town

Overview
Money Town is a project focused on economics and ethical discussions about money. This project requires a great deal of autonomy and initiative on the part of the students as Money Town is a fictional town where kids become immersed in role play around real world economics.

As this project is especially sensitive to the relationship between the teacher and her students, it should not be done in a classroom with a teacher who wields her power carelessly. It is not suited to a classroom where supplies have been withheld from children or where children are afraid to use supplies. This is a delicate project that could go astray given the wrong conditions or project leader. It is a project suited for a classroom where teacher and students can work playfully together and are used to working in democratic tandem rather than in an authoritarian power structure. It is primarily included here because it is an exceptional example of what children are capable of learning and understanding through experiential learning projects.

The teacher must be especially sensitive and aware of the needs and feelings of her students throughout the project and must be prepared to switch things up quickly to help ensure her students feel secure at every turn. That is not to say students shouldn't experience moments of struggle when trying to figure out solutions, but rather, they should always be feeling emotionally safe while immersed in a play scenario. They should be able to rely one hundred percent on a teacher who is able to readily "switch out" of her role play mode and back to her regular teacher mode. For that reason, it is a difficult project, and not one to be undertaken by someone inexperienced or unwilling or unable to do the delicate work of play.

Goals
By participating in a town simulation, students gain a fundamental understanding of economic principles as they begin to "make sense" of real-world economic systems through play scenarios and ongoing discussion, conflict and resolution, problem solving, and reflection.

Time Frame/Age Group
This is a one-to-two-week, short term project, appropriate for all ages of elementary students.

Materials
- School/classroom/play money and coins or an agreed upon currency
- TV tray tables (These are not a must, but they come in really handy as they make fantastic "pop-up" shops. The wooden ones work well as they are very stable.)
- Other supplies will vary according to student needs.

Preparation/Difficulty Level: Hard

This project is actually very easy and requires little to no prep. It is listed as difficult because it requires a great deal of imagination and tolerance along with a high level of "comfort with messiness" on the part of the teacher or project manager. This project is not for those needing to know outcomes before starting a project. It's unwieldy, completely follows student interests, and can become quite complicated and even a bit raucous. That said, this is also one of the most powerful projects contained in this book as it is packed full of student learning and "sensemaking".

Layout and Design

This project begins very simply, but you will need to be prepared for several areas of the classroom to be taken over by children wanting to turn it into a shop or center of their own design. Strip down the classroom of excess materials as best you can to make room for what's to come. The next step is to be prepared with several classroom jobs in mind for eager students looking for work.

The primary reason for stripping down the classroom of excess materials is that the project begins when you feel like the students might need a gentle lesson in the reality of the cost of materials. Maybe they've been taking the endless supply of classroom paper or replacement pencils for granted. Maybe they've not been caring for classroom materials as best as they could or helping to clean up the classroom lately. Maybe it's time for... Money Town.

Scaffolding

The project begins spontaneously when someone asks you for more of a school supply that has been frequently replaced or wasted, like tape or paper. Surprise them one day by saying, "Sure, but (a small stack of) paper now costs two "classroom" dollars." The student will either palm you an imaginary two dollars or say they don't have two "classroom" dollars. Take their imaginary money and wait for word to get around. It won't be long for the next student to ask for something else to see what you say. Repeat the statement and when they acknowledge they don't have any "classroom" money, tell them there are classroom jobs available where they can earn some (school/classroom/play) money, if they are interested. Watch their eyes light up after they slowly realize "the game is afoot".

Cleaning up and sorting classroom materials are great jobs to start off with and students can work them easily for a few minutes for three play money "classroom" dollars. They pay you two for the supply of paper they wanted and can keep a dollar for themselves. Wait for the electricity to move throughout the room as word gets around. "Money Town" has officially begun.

Suddenly everyone will either be looking for supplies or jobs. Be ready with lots of little classroom type jobs for students to work and start talking about ways kids can earn money within the classroom. Maybe someone wants to start working in the classroom Library. You, as the "Government", will provide the funding for that job. You don't particularly need to explain the concept of Government – it will be accepted as part of the game. Everything is a bit freewheeling and playful. Watch the "Town" become a hive of commerce in no time as students take initiative and dream up new jobs and roles.

Someone will eventually come up with the idea of having a store; maybe it's an art store or origami store, or whatever they dream up. They may decide to rent a space from you for a pretend dollar, or whatever amount of unit of currency you have decided to use in your Money Town. If there are too many students asking for spaces, suggest someone open a real estate agency and take charge of the transactions and parceling out of areas. Be prepared for lots of electricity as students begin to imagine new businesses. Everything is free flowing and moving fast. Don't get too hung up or rigid about exacting costs of supplies, or do, but keep it fun and at an achievable level for students as they begin to play within this new scenario.

Once again, the Bank provides a central and key role to the project as students can work there and take ownership of the

Banking system. Bankers can keep track of individual accounts, managing their classmates' withdrawals and deposits. Pay days can initially come from you, as the central bank, at an equal rate of five units per day, or you can differentiate between publicly funded positions and privately funded, where employers must pay their employees directly. You might decide to pay "5" units for general "work per day" or per job, depending on your preference. *It should go without saying that this is NOT ever paying students to do their academic work! The "work" is typical classroom-job type of jobs or of the students' own invention.* As project manager you may have to change the flow of money as student learning directions dictate.

Soon, flyers advertising people's stores may end up in the cubbies. This may lead to the need for some rules and regulations which may lead to the creation of a Post Office or lawmaker's Congressional job. (It is remarkable how quickly "junk mail" becomes a problem.) Once cash and commerce is flowing freely throughout the classroom, problems will arise. (It is also interesting to see how quickly that aspect develops when money is simply added into the mix of play!) Perhaps a Court spontaneously needs to be established with a Judge and defendants and plaintiffs represented by Lawyers. Guide on the side, but don't dictate; let them bang the gavel and object a bit. Ask a well-placed question or two. How will they know the law? Refer back to the laws that were created and passed by the Congress. In this way, slowly, students begin to gain an understanding of the exchange between the Legislative and Judicial branches of government as they interplay back and forth.

Should a Congress decide to convene, it is helpful to conduct sessions as a whole group so that everyone has a chance to hear the proposal of new rules. It also gives students a chance to catch up on what's been happening during each play session. You can introduce the "Congress" as a time to reflect on what happened during each "Money Town" play session. Frequent reflection time and open dialogue are key aspects of the project. As each student is automatically a member of their "Classroom Congress" (and therefore receives daily pay), it also helps students who may be hesitant or who do not have a job yet to secure funds.

Integrations
The different possibilities of businesses and directions this project can take are as limitless, as within society itself. Students should be coming up with ideas and teachers provide support, materials, and constant feedback through frequent dialogue with students. Kids will have a ton of ideas. Here are some to get started:

- The up/down money center: a simulated investment system where students can invest in specific stocks
- Lawyers, real estate agents, social work offices, and employment agencies
- Cleaning companies
- Post office, library, and bank
- Dance, yoga or exercise studios
- Performing arts or cultural spaces (These can be supplemented through governmental grants – that's you!)
- Scooter or classroom materials rental businesses (A business may "buy" a classroom commodity and then sell time or goods to classroom customers.)
- Cafes and various retail stores

Towards the end of the project, the "Government" might ask the citizens of Money Town to pay taxes. Create a tax form using whatever method supports your math curriculum; for example, if you are focused on addition, make that a primary calculation, or if you are working on percentage, ensure that calculation is part of the equation. Make sure students know what systems their taxes are going to support, whether that is government salaries, libraries, bank subsidies, arts and cultural grant supplements, or classroom supplies. It's also fun to use the pretend classroom tax money to purchase an actual classroom supply that benefits all the students as a way to celebrate the end of the project. A sample tax form is included in the "Resources and References" portion of this project outline.

A key aspect of this project is to, as the project gets rolling, spend time discussing the ethics of the money system within the town. For example, could and should the "Government" or a business charge for air or water? Ethical discussions should be occurring regularly and as an integral part of the project.

Additionally, incorporate "Money Town" scenarios into mathematical story problems and your regular math classes, as further support for students working with money in their regular academic classes.

Outcomes and Assessments

Here are some group observations made by second graders during the project:

- "People who work at the Bank... you have to earn the money. Money isn't free there."
- "People who are accountants, they learn to do the taxes."
- "People only go to that one store – the big store – and other people are like, "Only one person is at my store!" and that causes problems."
- "Raising the prices, instead of getting more money, you're actually losing it because the customer thinks the price is too high."
- "Someone is buying something at one store and then selling it for higher prices at their own store. They actually stole it from the store."
- "A lot of people get into fights about money."
- "We had crime and stealing."
- "As people start getting more money they start bragging about their money."

All these observations were made by children through their play – there was no "direct instruction" on any one topic, but rather a continuous flow of questions and answers between and among children and teacher during play. Documenting class discussions serves as an important reflection of what students are learning. Include group reflections along with students' individual written reflections as a final assessment piece. For individual assessments, depending on what topics came up and were explored during the scenario, some possible questions for students to write about or reflect on could include:

- What is the difference between public and private ownership?
- Are public goods important to towns and societies? Why or why not?
- Are banks important? Why or why not? What role do banks play in the town?
- What is the job of Congress? (Or your own country's law-making system?)
- Does Congress always make fair rules?
- Can you think of a law in the town that you thought was unfair? Or one that was needed and not there?
- How are problems solved in a town?
- What do lawyers do for people? What is the role of a Judge?
- How do price changes affect businesses? Do businesses change their prices? Why?
- What did you notice about friendships when money became a part of the town?
- Do you think it's a good idea for kids to learn about how money works in a town? Why or why not?
- What did you notice about how much some jobs were paid? Were some jobs harder than others? Were those jobs paid the same, less, or more?
- Are jobs that don't pay as much money important to the town? Why or why not?
- What are taxes? Are they important to the town? Why or why not?

Troubleshooting

Introducing the concept of money into a pretend town definitely opens up a "can of worms" and will impact the regular peaceful vibe and flow of play. Most of the issues that arise can be solved through introducing more play. For example, if there is a problem, a business owner can take the case to Court or bring it to Congress. However, teachers must ALWAYS be prepared to step in and intervene should they go too far.

Any emergence of crime should threaten to shut the project down should it continue. The play should not be allowed to extend into "jail" as it could cause distress to students. It is essential that conversations around ethics, justice, and economics are constantly taking place throughout the project. It also helps to limit the project to two weeks.

Extensions

Varying the pay for different jobs helps build in understanding of supply and demand, as well as concepts of economic justice, as students realize that, oftentimes, many of the essential jobs and roles may not be the most profitable. To build in deeper understandings and subtleties, you can differentiate between "owning" a location and "renting" a location as well as introducing loan and grant applications for various businesses and cultural organizations.

Additionally, introducing a miniature "Up/Down Stock Market" can add some spark to things, depending on student interests. They can choose to invest an amount into a company of their choice. Use actual data from daily stock trades on Wall Street to proportionally add or subtract amounts to their investment. It doesn't have to be exact! People can become brokers to help run the system. Keep it simple and playful as they begin to make sense of stock variability and investing.

Resources

Sample Student Tax Form

Name: _____
Grade: _____
Age: ___
Birthday Month: _____
Birthday Date: _____
Birthday Month + Date = Tax owed (line A) _____
Grade + Age = Standard deduction (line B) _____

A − B = Total tax owed _____
Additional deductions: (itemize and make-up as needed)
1. _____
2. _____

Total tax due including deductions: _____
Total tax refund: _____

Signed: _____
Payment or refund receipt: _____

3

Civics and Society

Philosophy and Application

As in the previous chapter, these projects are all designed to be playful, student-directed simulations and experiences that are enriched through teacher guidance and leadership. As with any experiential project, there is a "messiness" to them that some may find uncomfortable at first, though that uncertainty improves with practice and experience. These projects ask students to experiment, play, take initiative, and become deeply engaged with an aspect of the project and then to reflect upon their experience through a presentation or individual or collective piece of writing.

As standards vary from place to place, specific standards are not included within the confines of each of these projects, as they would be too numerous to list. For this chapter, a general topic list is provided for you next to each project to help you see how each can function in a cross-curricular fashion, as each project addresses numerous standards. This cross-curricular approach forms a much more efficient way of achieving sophisticated educational goals in a much smaller span of time. While it may take a few years of repeating a project to be able to fully list the array of objectives each accomplishes, it can be done on a continuum as you gain experience managing the width and breadth of each project.

Math and literacy, integrated with social studies, are presented first. Finally, as the three solely social studies projects outlined in this chapter are the most difficult projects in practice, they are listed last to help build understanding, as one project can build on the next.

Math and Social Studies Projects

This first series of projects highlight the integration of math with social studies. Keep in mind these projects are not intended to form the entirety of your math program but are designed to plug in to curriculums to enhance learning and engagement while showcasing mathematics in practice.

Tic Tac Toe Tournament

Social studies: building culture and community
　Math: logic and game theory

Overview
This is a mathematical game-based project that works well with K-5 students, either as a whole community or in individual classes.

Goal
The goal is for students to develop and strengthen skills involving problem solving, strategic planning, and logic, and to introduce and explore the concept of game theory. A secondary goal is to develop good sportsmanship within playing games.

Time Frame/Age Group
This project can take anywhere from a few days interspersed throughout the year to a four-week intense study. It is appropriate for grades K-5.

Materials
♦ To create the game, you can use paper and pencil, physical objects and board, or create digital versions.

Preparation Time/Level of Difficulty: Easy
The great thing about this project is that it can be as easy as you like, or you can extend it to include much more complexity. All you need is a few tic tac toe boards, which can be as simple as a drawing on paper, or "fancier" versions with physical "X"s and "O"s. The most difficult aspect of this project is developing fair and predictable tournament play. As multiple games can be completed at a rapid pace, it can be difficult to keep brackets accurate. Luckily, children are forgiving of imperfection, and it can actually help reduce the "competitiveness" when there's a bit of a messiness to the actual matchups. Among most any school community there's usually someone who is a bracket aficionado, so ask for help or, better yet, have older students develop an equitable system of matchups, which can be a whole project within itself!

Layout and Design
Many may balk at the "easiness" of tic tac toe for elementary-school-aged children, but you will be surprised at how frequently even older elementary students are not yet skilled in this area. Too often adults skip right to prepping children for chess without allowing them the time to mathematically explore simpler games. Children need time develop the ability to "look ahead" and see the consequences of their actions and to construct strategies based on active game play.

Be sure to focus on teaching students to win and lose gracefully, as that forms core "soft skills" around game play within a community. It's an important skill for children to know how to win and how to lose. Tic tac toe is a great way to address so many interpersonal skills, as game play is rapid and the stakes are low.

Scaffolding
The other great thing about this project is that it can take place within one classroom or many at a time and often transcends ages,

meaning that skilled seven-year-olds can be competitive against ten-year-olds. Start small with in-class partners playing a series of games and then talk about it as a class afterwards. Then, you can expand to include other classrooms or have your tournament winners play in other classrooms. The great thing here is that you can organize tournament play as easy or as complex as desired. Here's a sample list of what skills each grade can focus on:

- Kindergarten: taking turns (It's not that they can't learn to play, but it's more that this is the desired skill outcome.)
- 1st grade: rules of game play
- 2nd grade: lots of practice, predicting outcomes
- 3rd grade: being able to explain strategy, predicting outcomes, developing alternate representations of X and O, fair play, sportsmanship
- 4th/5th grade: designing game play online, analyzing game play, constructing models of every possible outcome, exploring game theory, extrapolating to other games

Integrations

Math is the biggie here, but you can integrate your physical education department by incorporating more serious tournament play or even by creating giant games of live tic tac toe, which may help some students be able to literally see the "bigger picture". Integrate technology by developing online games through coding or digital applications and by having students generate possibilities and outcomes for games.

Outcomes and Assessments

Treating a seemingly simple game like tic tac toe as a serious and valid mathematical project will yield some unexpected and interesting results. Another great reason why tic tac toe is such a wonderful project is the breadth of built-in differentiation and the versatility of assessment:

- Regularly documenting whole group conversations surrounding strategy development can form the cornerstone of assessing what students discovered about the game.

- One-on-one interviews or small group meetings with students who are in similar areas of development can also be helpful to evaluate students' observations and insights.
- Small group or partner presentations on what they've developed or discovered through game play can serve as a final assessment for the project.
- Individual project presentations can be incorporated for more advanced students who have delved into outcome analysis, game theory or have developed more complex game boards.

Troubleshooting

Most of the difficulty arises if you are running tournaments, which gets easier with practice or by using online bracket generators, or by being forgiving of yourself and others for not being one hundred percent accurate in the matchups. Ask for help from someone with skill in this area if need be!

Extensions

Game play can morph into Sudoku, 3D versions of tic tac toe, checkers, Connect Four, Battleship, chess or any game of strategy or logic. There are ways to create more complexity within the project:

- Involve students in developing fair and accurate tournament brackets.
- Students can referee and record outcomes in games for younger students.
- Analyze the number of possible outcomes for games and the least number of turns in which a game can be won.
- Develop game trees to figure out every possibility of play for each move.
- Students can develop their own online versions of the tic tac toe or other game board.

Resources

Chambers, Andrew Game theory and Tic Tac Toe. *ibmathsresources.com*, November 24, 2013. https://ibmathsresources.com/2013/11/24/game-theory-and-tic-tac-toe/

Weisstein, Eric W. Tic-Tac-Toe. *From mathworld--A wolfram web resource.* https://mathworld.wolfram.com/Tic-Tac-Toe.html

RISK and Gamer Teams

Social studies: geography
   Math: probability, logic, statistics

Overview
This game-based project is specifically geared towards the *RISK* board game made by Hasbro, but the same approach can be used for other high-level games, like *Diplomacy*, *Civilization*, or *Age of Empires*. The *RISK* board game incorporates educational possibilities for diplomacy, statistics, probability, strategy, geography, and history.

Goals
Through the sustained inquiry of a gaming experience, students will develop a research question or project based on game play. Questions might revolve around:

- How geography affects war (historical and contemporary)
- Developing a working understanding of probability through recording dice rolls
- Recording successive moves and their rates of success/failure
- A discussion of diplomatic, cooperative, and game playing skills and strategies
- Strategies and maps of potential outcomes/approaches
- Research of specific historical battle maps and how they may or may not apply to game play
- Developing alternate maps
- Researching details and information about specific battles, wars, and generals

Time Frame/Age Group
This is a four-to-six-week project best suited for children aged 12 and up. While most of the projects listed in this book are for

K-5 elementary students, this project shows how game play can be incorporated into curriculums for older grades. While the complexity of this gameplay is prime for children aged 12- 18, this project is suitable for some groups of 10-year-olds. You can change the board game as needed, but it should be one that has a large enough degree of challenge, complexity, and relevancy that it can provide sustained inquiry and deep research opportunities for students.

Materials
You can use one board game, but it's nice to have multiple copies of the same board game (look for used ones); if using the *RISK* game, find additional large historical and current maps and extra gaming pieces. The app is a fantastic option but requires a tablet or app-accessible technology and there are a lot of in-game purchase options, which may eventually become an issue in the classroom environment as they don't currently support or offer classroom deals for education.

Preparation Time/Difficulty Level: Medium
Most of your preparation time is in securing the physical board games and ensuring YOU know how to play, which is essential for any gaming project. Log some gametime with a group of friends or online to learn how to play, if you don't already know how to. Once you have the physical board games, the project is largely a matter of fostering extensions to the actual game play. Using the game *RISK* makes a nice curricular companion to a historical study of specific battles, so you will also need to be prepared to make connections between game play and whatever historical battles you choose to feature for discussion.

Layout and Design
While this game-based project can become a bit unwieldy in its ability to spark passionate play, there are huge opportunities for learning as students are given the opportunity to create roles outside of immediate game play. While it may take time for players to learn how to play, one game will be enough for students to be able to develop questions for further inquiry. Game play

and inquiry work in tandem as students and teachers change scenarios, maps, and teams to help explore game variables. Final projects could involve students sharing research results, creating movies or documentaries, showcasing their own historical or current maps, or holding seminars on diplomacy using examples from history, within game play or in current events.

Scaffolding

- To start, use one game board and have teams consist of multiple players who must make collective decisions and moves. This is a good way to build community between players, develop team building and to begin to learn gameplay. *RISK* is a six-player game, so one game board can accommodate 24 students in four-person teams.
- When beginning the gameplay, stop regularly during play to have students write and discuss. *RISK* is a game that can get quite passionate, so this will help regularly lower the temperature. Be prepared to share your observations and openly discuss strategy, problems, or connections you notice through your observations. These conversational breaks will also help students begin to select a specific inquiry project based on the game.
- You can also start games and stop them mid-play and have other teams pick up the play. This may allow for a reduction in the "ownership" of a certain color, strategy or game and force students to see strategies from different perspectives.

Integrations

History and geography play big roles in this project as you can incorporate map making, historical maps, and research of historical battles. Math has a significant role here as well, as students can focus on the probability of winning dice rolls. The app has 80 different maps to choose from, which can inform and inspire both your content and your students.

Outcomes and Assessments

Assessment for this game project is student presentations on their chosen aspect of the game. Some ideas are:

- Create a book of tips for game play.
- Develop a record of dice rolls and outcomes.
- Draw maps of historical battles.
- Create detailed strategy maps from various attack locations.
- Research and present tips on diplomacy and/or major peace agreements, both historically and from the game.
- Recount gameplays in detail.
- Make a list of longitude and latitude coordinates for key locations.
- Create new adaptations and variations of gameplay.

Troubleshooting

As anyone who has played this game in college or with family or friends can attest, this game can get heated and passionate. This will be the primary difficulty and you will have to work hard to head off blow-ups before they occur by reducing the temperature of gameplay through mixing up teams, keeping the games moving and ensuring that regular whole-group troubleshooting discussions are core to the project. Additionally, lean into the controversies and foster procedures to address conflicts. Can a game of world domination create a functioning variation of the United Nations?

Extensions

- Try having multiple game boards in-play simultaneously. Students can play alone or with a partner and represent colors. If you have four games going simultaneously, have all the "Yellows" or "Blues" meet together intermittently during game play to strategize and compare notes.
- Encourage students to explore specializing in certain strategies (for example, the "Australia strategy", the "South American strategy") and to record their moves based on gaming.

Resources

- Create a form so students can list each of the countries according to whatever continent it is associated with.

- ♦ Create forms for students to record dice rolls.
- ♦ Use maps to have students document moves and strategies.

RISK: Game of Global Domination, board game by Hasbro, app by SMG Studio for Hasbro.

Math Court

Social studies: focus on civics

Math: process standards as outlined by the National Council of Teachers of Mathematics and Standards for Mathematical Practice within Common Core State Standards in the United States

Overview
This is a play-based experiential project designed to help students learn about the judicial system, where students begin to defend their thinking, prove cases, and engage in healthy debate designed to arrive at truth.

Goals
The goal is for students to present and defend math problems through proofs, logical thinking and respectful and procedural conversation that mirrors court procedures.

Time Frame/Age Group
This project is suitable for Grade 2 and up. You can apply this project structure at various times throughout the year as needed. The actual court sessions are short – about five to fifteen minutes of class time, as needed.

Materials
No specific materials are needed, but a judge's gavel will go a long way. Meat tenderizers or playdough mallets will do very well.

Preparation/Difficulty Level: Easy
No specific preparation needs to take place for this project; it is more a culture that needs to have been established before you

can freely slip in and out of "play mode" with your class, as discussed in the first chapter of this book. Whenever you feel the class is ready, the project can begin with little to no introduction. Starting with a simple, formal, "So, Counselor Marcus, you are claiming that two and two is four, can you prove that beyond a reasonable doubt?" Watch students quickly try to figure out what you are talking about, then suddenly realize you have entered a playful zone. Give a little wink and nod to show you know that they know and voilà – the game's afoot! Marcus will doubt himself for a blink of an eye, but then realize he can ABSOLUTELY prove that two and two is four! This is an official inquiry now and "case closed": Marcus has stated his case very well and proven that two and two do indeed make four. It is important to start with problems you are sure your students can solve easily to help them develop confidence as you playfully fold this structure into your weekly mathematical routine.

Layout and Design

It's important to start this project slowly and build in more formality as the students become more comfortable with the idea of publicly proving their answers and sharing their thinking. Most mathematical school communities are well versed in these types of routines, but introducing the pretend court setting can add a layer of intimidation for some. It is essential that you, as teacher and now pretend judge, are aware and sensitive to students' hesitations and reservations and ensure that they are successful in their first attempts to help them build confidence in their skills as mathematical litigators. It should go without saying that beyond any game, project, skill, or concept, it is paramount that you ALWAYS give students a way to save face and to be successful.

With that all said, "Math Court" can evolve as both you and your students "play together" at co-constructing this routine for checking math problems together. Someone may want to take on the role of bailiff and announce "All Rise" when math court convenes. Court works particularly well for story problems, as students present their evidence, which may result in another student providing evidence to the contrary. For story problems, slow down and take time to prove cases in order:

1. logical procedures, "I knew to subtract because…"
2. resulting calculations
3. any statements of additional conclusion

While one student states her case, you as judge should ask if anyone can confirm her case or can offer evidence to the contrary. Ask the pretend jury if they all agree and close that case. When someone disagrees, they can state their case in court. Sessions don't have to be long; the idea is that court is where we sometimes come together to talk about and prove math cases. Court should last no more than five to fifteen minutes of each class period.

While each individual "math court" session is not a project in itself, strung together over time, these playful sessions form the foundation for a final presentation where students present a portfolio of their work in the "math court" setting. Each of the short sessions leading up to the final project not only helps build student understanding of mathematics, but a better sense of understanding of the judicial system. Using whole class "Math Court" meetings in tandem with the next project listed in this chapter, "Math Debate Teams", meld the two structures together to help form a solid system in which students can begin to develop their sense of the judicial branch of government.

Scaffolding
The strength of this structure is that you can fold it in as often as you like, introducing it when a particularly challenging math problem comes up, or use it to help reluctant students gain more confidence in presenting their thinking. In your regular math sessions when you see a student do something particularly interesting or there is a disagreement about an answer or procedure, ask them if they'd like to present it in court and begin the "formal" procedures.

Integrations
It is rare for curriculums to find driving relationships between math and social studies. This project makes it crystal clear that not only are there intersections, but the two disciplines are in core relationships with one another as, together, they help form the backbone of the judicial system.

The beauty of play, imagination, and experiential learning applied to math here is that you don't need to go into long descriptions or lessons about the judicial system, rather, you just slowly immerse students into the structure and adjust the reality of the experience as needed. Students will immediately make connections between your invented court procedures and see that court is a place for truth and to prove cases. You can then use their knowledge to help them build their understanding of the role of Congress, cases of injustice, or new freedoms for those wronged or landmark cases.

Outcomes and Assessments
The strength of this approach is that it helps students slow down and recognize and identify both the multiple errors and valid approaches that can be made along the way to solving mathematical problems. The court method helps students develop critical thinking skills and helps prioritize the concept of "truth seeking" when it comes to mathematics.

Again, while this is not in itself a "project" it is an important piece of immersive, playful, but real experiential learning that leads to students being confident and capable when they deliver their final year-long math project in "court". The digital components of the final math project are outlined in the last chapter of this book, but you can tailor and construct differentiated "final cases" for individual students to verbally solve in "court" as a way to showcase their learning. Presenting digitally works well here as you can easily invite their parents or other guests to attend virtually, as is outlined more specifically in Chapter Five.

Troubleshooting
While students may hesitate to speak out at first, adding the imaginative component of the court helps give students confidence

and drive to "know", and to "solve the case". As their fear of "being wrong" dissipates and they view themselves on a journey to "find truth", some of the competitiveness of math yields towards a more cooperative approach. This is where the application of "Math Debate Teams", as outlined next, becomes an essential part of building your mathematical community.

Another bit of troubleshooting is that the routine can become tiresome for children if it is used too much or too vigorously. This is one project where the adult could easily become semantic, too tied to reality, and overly concerned with the rules, losing sight of the fact that it is enough for the game to be played very simply and gently.

Extensions

This general foundation of understanding can then be applied to a more elaborate project more focused on social studies, which is outlined later in this chapter. Additionally, you can take a field trip to the courthouse, interview judges or lawyers, bailiffs, clerks, or other positions of the court. A thorough extension of this project is explained in the next section of this chapter.

Resources

Website: *Council of Chief State School Officers, Common Core State Standards.* https://learning.ccsso.org/wp-content/uploads/2022/11/Math_Standards1.pdf

Website: *National Council of Teachers of Mathematics.* https://www.nctm.org/

Math Debate Teams

Social studies: civics

Math: process standards as outlined by the National Council of Teachers of Mathematics and Standards for Mathematical Practice within Common Core State Standards in the United States

Overview
This is a problem-based team project where students work in small-group cooperative math teams focused on arriving at "truth" and reaching "consensus" in mathematical problems. The imaginative play aspect of this project is that students are "in training" as "lawyers" in the Math Court as they work these math exercises in logic to help prove their cases.

Goals
Students engage in respectful dialogue and debate with peers regarding explanations of their mathematical thinking, with the goal being that students become more adept at detecting mathematical errors, checking over their work and defending their logic in service of truth.

Time Frame/Age Group
This is a full year project, better suited to older elementary children in grades 2 and up.

Materials
There are no extra materials needed besides regular math program materials, though adding cooperative gaming as a regular feature to the teams is a great addition. There are many options for cooperative board games. A resource we especially like is https://cooperativegames.com/ from Suzanne Lyons.

Preparation/Difficulty Level: Easy
Participation in a few whole-class "Math Court" sessions, as explained in the previous pages, opens children up to the idea of role playing and "acting out" a court scenario where they learn there is a judge, and you must defend thinking with proof. You don't need to go into a lot of detail; children are eager to play along and generally have limited experience with the judicial system, so there's a lot of grace available to you as you bumble through the playful scenario. If you do have children who have had negative experiences with the judicial system, shelve this project for another year. Meant to be a playful project, you don't want to cause distress to a child who may have had previous

traumatic associations with court. Always use your best judgment as to what works best for your students. This "math court" is intended to be fun, playful and core to learning math. Though most students have shadowy knowledge of a court setting, they are eager to play and participate in a pretend scenario as you slowly craft and build their knowledge through the experience.

Layout and Design

This project can stand alone or work in tandem with the "Math Court" project as previously described. The structure for this project is fairly simple: it's basically cooperative math teams of four working together to agree on one answer. What's different and of key importance to the project is the addition of the playful context of court and lawyers in relation to mathematics.

Mathematics often has little contextual relationship to the real world. Students NEED to, and are always looking to, make sense of what they are learning whether we provide them with it or not. Mathematics, for the most part, are essentially exercises in a language of logic. Let that statement sink in for a bit and realize that so much of what we teach in elementary school mathematics is not actually math at all, but rather simply PROCEDURES or recipes. Thinking of math as "exercises in the language of logic" should really change the game for many teachers and – most importantly – KIDS!

Who needs logic? Detectives solving cases, lawyers, people trying to solve mysteries and puzzles of the unknown, and people who need to prove their case to the world. THAT'S why algebra. THAT'S why geometry. They are problems and exercises of the mind and brain to help humans become more logical and be able to express that logic through the language of mathematics. That framing not only makes sense to children, it deeply motivates them. They are given a contextual frame of mathematics and a window of opportunity as they begin to view "being wrong" not as failure but as an opportunity for discovery and success. Additionally, leadership skills are being consistently built through their work in the cooperative groupings.

Keep groups moving as needed, ideally every four weeks, but if you have personality conflicts or need to pair up certain children at certain times, groups can move more frequently. Either way, it is important to move them regularly, as fresh groupings produce new opportunities.

Scaffolding

The primary groundwork you need to do involves teaching respectful dialogue and getting students to set aside their personal attachments to being in the "right" or in the "wrong". Depending on your class, this will be difficult or easy and may be a slow process to develop. It is not easy for anyone, especially children, to admit an error, but focus on modeling that "the math" is when a student can FIND THE ERROR. Emphasize over and over that finding errors is like getting a gold star in math. Mean it, be serious about it, and reward it. Humans are going to make errors; it is part of being human. Success in math, life, or in court is when you can detect one. Here are some tips for talking to children about making and admitting errors:

- ♦ Humans make errors so often there's actually an expression called "human error".
- ♦ Miscounting is an extremely common error to make. Miscounting is so common you may want to consider checking your counting strategy with another strategy.
- ♦ Mathematicians always double check their answers.
- ♦ You might have a group where three friends say the answer is six and one might say the answer is eight and the answer might be eleven and so they are all wrong.
- ♦ In that same scenario, if you are the one student who thinks it might be eight, recognize that this might be the correct answer; just because more students believe it's six, it doesn't make it true.
- ♦ When we think about voting and democracy, the most votes win, but in math, truth wins. Like math, court is about arriving at truth.
- ♦ When you make a mistake, how do you feel? Should anyone brag or be unkind when that happens? You can form some class codes of ethics around these scenarios as needed.

♦ This is your math TEAM. They are there to help you and work with you; you are one team together. It's OK to be wrong and make mistakes with them.

Integrations
This project works particularly well in service of checking homework, for several reasons:

♦ It holds students accountable to their team versus the teacher or the subject matter.
♦ Homework is a bit "lower stakes" in terms of ego.
♦ Teams keep each other in check; homework is essentially self-checked through a structured error finding community.
♦ Students can progress quickly through checking or, if there are common problems, those can be brought to "Math Court."
♦ Students develop cooperative skills in organizing themselves into highly functioning groups who can complete tasks quickly.

Outcomes and Assessments
This play project facilitates numerous skills essential for students as they:

♦ are slowly freed up from the fear of "being bad at math"
♦ see that errors are inevitable and they become more capable of admitting one
♦ become more adept at error detection as they check and recheck calculations
♦ approach math as truth-seeking exercises with logical proofs versus "correctness"
♦ gain experience disagreeing, debating, and leading teams
♦ become more articulate in explaining mathematical reasoning
♦ are held accountable to their teams.

The final assessment of this project comes at the end of the year when a child is given a math problem to solve and does so in a court of math, with a jury of peers, parents, and/or school staff. The student can present their particular case as part of a larger "math portfolio", which we talk about more extensively in Chapter Five, "Working Together in a Digital World". No matter the audience, the final assessment showcases each student's ability to publicly talk about their process and approach to the math problem and share any difficulties they may have encountered along the way.

Troubleshooting

Passionate group arguments, hurt feelings or one student in a group not participating will make up most of any difficulty encountered in this project. That is where the civics piece does so much heavy lifting for you as the issues that arise in "reaching consensus" mirrors so much of the political process. Another advantage of incorporating civics is that unlike politics or democracy, there is a clear truth in math. This can help that student who has a lot of passion and powers of persuasion, but little skill, begin to slow down and look at the problem as well as giving students with high skill the challenge to articulate their proofs to peers. It's fascinating to see what blooms from the structure of these functioning teams working together. Note teams need consistent attention from you as you work to carefully scaffold in each piece.

Extensions

In terms of play, you can also frame teams as "detectives" who are working cases towards becoming lawyers or just a badge. Get into it with theme songs (The "Night Court" theme song is a favorite) and have kids adopt regular jobs like bailiff. Announce the page numbers in your math workbook as "dockets" and the individual problem number as the "cases". Be playful, be serious, have a good time and prove those cases!

Math teams ensure you will always have built in groupings for other activities should you need. Additionally, groups might enjoy creating their own names or identities should there be enough time.

Resources

Council of Chief State School Officers, Common Core State Standards. https://learning.ccsso.org/wp-content/uploads/2022/11/Math_Standards1.pdf

New York State Next Generation Mathematics Learning Standards. (2017). http://www.nysed.gov/common/nysed/files/programs/curriculum-instruction/nys-next-generation-mathematics-p-12-standards.pdf

Expanding Circles: Places

Social studies: geography
  Math: geometry, measurement

Overview

An "Expanding Circles" design project is where students are challenged to study and reproduce buildings, towns, and increasingly larger spheres of geographic regions through an architectural research and mapping study using various materials. Students create both models and maps of locations and physical structures. This serves as a companion project to the "Portraits and Interviews" project outlined later in this chapter, as that project focuses on people and this project focuses on places.

Goals

The goal is for students to build and create accurate representations of buildings, monuments, bridges, or real-life structures using representational materials that include mathematical language, geometric terms and beginning concepts of scale, as is age appropriate.

Time Frame/Age Group

This project can be a four-to-six-week project or a full year study accessible for all ages. This makes an exceptional "spiraling project", as alternate aged grades can reflect the developmental stages of their work, especially in regard to showcasing children's representational and mathematical abilities.

Materials
Blocks, blocks, and more blocks! The traditional hard wooden unit blocks found in any kindergarten or early childhood program are ideal, though there are many different types of building and constructing materials designed for educational uses that would be interesting and appealing to students. Alternatively, if you don't have wooden blocks, you can use paper or cardboard to construct 3D buildings or simply draw representations.

Preparation/Difficulty Level: Medium
What makes this project tricky is the amount of space needed to construct and display designs. Limiting construction and display times and documenting the work through photographs can help.

Additionally, if you can attend workshops at the *City and Country School in New York*, they are a primary source to draw from as Caroline Pratt, a teacher and founder of the school, designed unit blocks and created a specific model of working with the blocks that is essential learning for every elementary mathematics educator. The block creations that the young children at the school create are absolutely incredible and worth your time and attention. A link to their website is included at the end of this project.

Layout and Design
This project hinges on the concept of "expanding circles", as students begin the project by building block representations of significant areas of the school building, beginning with their own classroom. Students construct block representations or any type of 3D model of their own learning space. From there, the circle can expand to include the cafeteria, gym, entrance of the school, etc., to finally include an entire representative model of the school building.

Students can even begin by constructing representations of the furniture around them and expand out to building models and maps of the classroom. Wherever you decide to begin, the idea is that children look closely at their immediate spaces and focus on the shapes, lines, and sizes they see and work to represent them as accurately as possible through whatever method is decided upon. From there, expand out to other spaces and model those. After the school has been represented, look to place the school in context of the town or city and the town or city in context of the landscape and larger area surrounding that, so that eventually the school has "shrunk" in proportion to larger areas. Have students work to represent those circles through mapping exercises.

Each project is photographed to help preserve the design and then incorporated into the next layer of design so that students build greater context of proportion and space (and so you won't run out of blocks or space!) As children age, their designs will naturally become more technical and truer to size, shape, and form. The closer they begin to look at details, the more they will begin to naturally lean into applying concepts of measurement, geometry, and proportion.

After students represent spaces using 3D blocks, or if you are short on blocks, have them work to draw the structure or space, creating a flat visual of their representation. They can also use computer simulation modeling to do this, should you have access to such programs. The point is to have them document their work before it is taken down and made into the next iteration. In a nutshell:

- Look closely at your first item to build or draw. It could be a chair or one area in the classroom.
- Work to represent through 3D modeling with tangible objects like blocks.
- Students draw their buildings or work to create more accurate drawings.
- The work is photographed.
- Repeat the same process with the next, larger space.
- Showcase the first series of drawings while beginning the next set of representations.

Scaffolding

Starting small, such as building representations of furniture, is a good starting point if you are looking to first keep the project on a smaller scale. Have students draw their plans and designs and give talks about their process. From there, expand out as you can. You can also coordinate with other grades and have them recreate sections of the school or larger area to make the project more manageable. Students can work in pairs, small teams or on their own as is decided.

Integrations
This project makes an excellent companion piece to "Portraits and Interviews", as you can have grades K, 2 and 4 focus on "people", while grades JK, 1, 3, and 5 focus on the idea of "place", uniting the entire project under a "People and Places" project. Having every other grade do a similar project is a great way to showcase the development that occurs throughout the rapid development of the elementary-school-aged child.

Outcomes and Assessments
The beauty of this project is that everyone is successful and works at their own level to push the limits of their own design. If you want to include more specific mathematical requirements, there is more than enough space within the project for you to do so. Work together with your class to decide what a successful outcome would look like. Whatever your specific requirements, students should be prepared to present and talk about the actual constructions or photographs of the work and be able to explain their design process along with relevant facts and details about their "in real life" building or area they chose to represent. Be sure to be clear and upfront with students about your expectations and requirements for what constitutes a successful project.

Troubleshooting
Getting your hands on a volume of building materials can be tricky, even in the best of circumstances. It may be beneficial to have small groups rotate through the project throughout a length of time. Other options include using cardboard boxes and recycled materials that can be repurposed to create small, scaled representations.

Extensions

Expand out to famous landmarks and buildings around the world. Include mapping and landscape as a functional part of the project, with teams coordinating between each other. Teams of older elementary students could try to use digital mapping and 3D programs to place buildings in perspective of cities and towns.

Resources

Mecabricks https://mecabricks.com/en/workshop
Tinkercad https://www.tinkercad.com/
SketchUp https://www.sketchup.com/
Google Earth
CBC Kids 3D Block Builder Game (free) https://www.cbc.ca/kids/games/all/3d-block-builder
City and Country School, Blocks Program. https://www.cityandcountry.org/programs/lower-school/blocks-program/
New York State Next Generation Mathematics Learning Standards (2017). http://www.nysed.gov/common/nysed/files/programs/curriculum-instruction/nys-next-generation-mathematics-p-12-standards.pdf

Literacy and Social Studies Projects

This next series of projects highlights the integration of literacy and social studies. While these projects are not intended to form the entirety of your literacy program, they can occur within literacy blocks of time, plug-in short-term projects, or as part of regular units of study.

Expanding Circles: People

Social studies: history, culture, and community
   Literacy: nonfiction study, narrative and informational writing and reading

Overview

This project focuses on the people of a community, beginning with a "circle" of the most immediate school community through a series of interviews and portraits. The circle continues to grow as people from the extended community are interviewed and drawn. This is a literacy, art, and social studies project that works well with any age group. This project makes an excellent companion project to the "Places" project previously outlined.

Goals

The goal of this project is for students to improve literacy, art, and leadership skills through conducting a series of interviews of members within communities and drawing their portraits. Student work is then presented to the community.

Time Frame/Age Group

The time frame can be adapted from two weeks to a full year project, depending on how many interviews or research pieces you decide to include in the project. Works with grades K-5 and up. This makes an exceptional "spiraling project", as alternate aged grades can reflect the developmental stages of their work, especially in regard to showcasing children's literacy and art.

Materials

- Forms with predetermined questions for interviews (These can be class or teacher generated.)
- 8.5 × 11 writing paper (or written on computer)
- 8.5 × 11 paper for portrait artwork
- Oil pastels for portraits (You can use crayons but oil pastels are much more vibrant.)
- 11 × 17 paper for mounting/displaying both pieces together

Preparation Time/Difficulty Level: Medium

This project doesn't take much in terms of preparation; the difficulty here is juggling all the multiple interviews. Arranging all the locations and timing and coordination of students visiting or sitting down with various school community members can be tricky at first, but it gets easier with practice.

It can also be time consuming and a bit chaotic managing the amount of physical paper and mounting all the portraits and written pieces together, but just keep at it and before you know it, it comes together. As with most every project in this book, it is a good idea to start small and build up the complexity over several years as you develop your own personal systems of project management.

Layout and Design

Focusing on the concept of "expanding circles of community", students use an interview form to ask questions to various sets of community members. After the interview, students use the form to help them construct short narrative pieces. You can pre-make the form or students can generate their own questions. Sample questions are provided for you at the end of this project outline.

The initial "circle" begins with themselves and then the "circles" expand to include other "sets" of community members. The structure of the concentric circles helps students build awareness of themselves within their community. The circles are color coded to help build clarity of the project's expansion and plan.

Community "circles" of interviews and portraits can be:

- All about me
- Classmates
- Other grade levels
- Adults who work within the school, including staff and administration
- Town shopkeepers, wait staff, cashiers, cooks, etc.
- Government or town employees, librarians, judges, town Mayor
- Non-profit leaders important to your town
- People of historic or cultural importance from your town who you research and read about (rather than conduct an interview with).

Scaffolding and Sequence

Students begin on the first few days of school filling out a questionnaire with details like their birthday, favorite color, favorite activity, and a few other casual "get to know you" type questions. They then take the questionnaire and "transcribe" the information from questions into narrative form. Finally, they draw a portrait of themselves, and the two pieces are mounted and presented together within a classroom art gallery. This is the first "circle" of the project.

The next circle expands to include the staff and teachers at the school who students interview using a similar pre-made form. After they interview their assigned person, they again "transcribe" into narrative form and draw their assigned member of staff or teacher's portrait. Assign each child a specific adult within the school community to interview. As time allows, you can also decide to expand and add another "circle" to include other classrooms, which is a nice way to forge connections between the student body or for older children to interview younger children. At the completion of the entire set, student work is presented in a community art show.

1. Students interview teachers/staff/students in other classes in person using the questionnaire form.
2. Transcribe it in class into narrative form.
3. Edit as needed.
4. Draw the portraits.
5. Mount together.
6. Display for show.

You can repeat this pattern for as large a circle as you can get in person and then move into having students read and research people and draw their portraits. As a field trip, take a walk through the town where your school is located and interview various people at shops, stores, and community and governmental organizations using the same format. For the town walk, you can also add in various people from "back then" of historical/cultural importance, and have students write up short biographies on those people and, finally, draw their portraits. Mount and present the work in a common space where the people the students interviewed can come and see the work.

Expand even larger and interview or do write-ups on people from your state or province. Mount the works on colorful paper for an in-person art gallery and then digitize the images and link them to the circles in a presentation format or create a school map directory of community members. The interviews and research do not have to be tomes or done perfectly – done well, it shows the developmental process and clear connection between art and writing.

Integrations

Art is the most obvious integration here and serves seamlessly as a study in portraiture. History comes in when studying community members from "back then". Easily fold the project into your literacy units on biography or narrative writing.

Outcomes and Assessments

One of the many strengths and outcomes of the project, besides developing literacy skills, is that students and schools engage in exchange with each other and the larger community. Sharing student work beyond school buildings and immediate physical spaces builds bridges and forges new relationships within communities.

The repetition of transcribing the form from question into narrative form helps hesitant writers have something to "hang onto", as they can copy some of the words from the interview questionnaire, while more advanced writers can work to add their own style and flair to the interview. Aim for students to complete three or four pieces of writing in three or four weeks so as not to belabor perfection of the piece, but rather to have students be engaged in the active practice of writing. For a formal assessment or outcome, you will have several pieces of writing that serve as a portfolio of evidence.

Troubleshooting

Most of the confusion comes from students getting the actual interviews. If your students are not allowed to independently move around the building on their own to go visit another classroom or school office, you will have to invite your school community to stop by your classroom, which may involve a student having to leave another lesson to secure the interview. It may be tough at first, but you will find it soon becomes a "controlled chaos" that finds its own sort of order.

Extensions
This project has been tested in second grade and would work well all the way through at least fifth grade (and even into adulthood – hello Oprah!)

- For children younger than second grade, stick to the "self" circle and have them try a paper cut-out representation of themselves with their name and some "fun facts about themselves" written alongside.
- To increase the difficulty for older students, increase the complexity of the interview questions.
- For older students, this could be done as a series of news stories or profiles.
- Use in tandem with the "Architecture Blocks" project in this book and have grades K, 2, and 4 focus on profiling "people" of the community, while grades PreK, 1, 3, and 5 focus on "place". Then, present the entire project separately, as pieces that slowly unfold throughout the year or culminate in one big extravaganza, or throughout the year.

Resources
Sample interview form questions:

- What is your name?
- What job do you do here?
- What is your favorite color? Animal? Thing to do? Book? Movie?
- What do you like about this community?
- What do you find scary?
- What do you wish this community had more of?
- What classes did you like when you were in school?

- What are you proud of?
- Can you share a memory or story from when you were a kid?

Council of Chief State School Offices, Common Core State Standards, US. https://learning.ccsso.org/wp-content/uploads/2022/11/ELA_Standards1.pdf

The Neighborhood Newspaper

Social studies: civics, culture and community, history, geography
Literacy: non-fiction and research skills, opinion writing
Math: data collection and organization
Science: weather, nature, animals

Overview

This is a community-based literacy project focused on nonfiction writing and research skills. Social studies concepts are addressed through the evaluation of sources and materials within the nonfiction study. The project includes student planning of tracking circulation and delivery of the newspaper to subscribers. This project also works well in conjunction with the "The School of Citizens" project, outlined later in this chapter.

Goals

The goal is for students to develop literacy skills within nonfiction reading and writing. Students create community through regular, frequent, and predictable newspaper circulation. Foster exchange between students writing for real audiences and community members seeing authentic children's work.

Time Frame/Age Group

Publish one newspaper a week for six weeks. The project is suitable for grades 2 and up.

Materials

- Students will need access to computers and Google Docs or another word processing program.

- Teacher access to Google Docs, or another word processing program with the ability to convert final products to a PDF format, or alternative publishing program.
- 11.5 × 17 paper if the newspaper is being photocopied and printed for distribution.

Preparation Time/Difficulty Level: Hard

What makes this project difficult is:

- Pace: the goal of publishing one full paper a week is ambitious, but doable. To start, try publishing one paper every two weeks.
- The amount of time it takes you, as both editor in chief and typesetter, to assemble the bits and pieces of student writing into a cohesive and attractive format. You will gain new appreciation for how actual newspapers are created as you work at a rapid pace to fit Susie's piece on sloths next to Cara's extensive hand drawn weather report. Get comfortable with formatting.
- All this is done while simultaneously helping a class of children with the mechanics of writing and researching nonfiction pieces.
- If you are not working digitally, getting resources can be tricky.

The most essential piece of preparation for this project is having a digital classroom or system at the ready where students can access a wide variety of sites for research on everything from sports to weather to world news. Chapter Five in this book talks extensively about how to create a digital template for this type of project. Having done this project both with and without a digital classroom, be assured it is greatly improved when students are able to independently access resources digitally. Work with your librarian to help you assemble LOTS of resources on a vast number of topics for students to go to find information either online or through physical materials. Be prepared to be constantly updating and editing those resources according to student interests.

The other thing to prepare for ahead of time is the look of the paper and how it will be presented. Take some time getting comfortable with your chosen method of publishing. Nothing fancy is needed; Google Docs works very well as it is easy to access student work through Google Classroom or shared documents – you can simply cut and paste student work into the newspaper template. To make a template, after you've designed the header banner, create a 2 × 1 table and experiment with formats authentic to a newspaper style. This may take some time, so be prepared with your format before you go into the project so you can focus on the students once you've launched.

Another thing to consider is how the paper will be published. Digital only? Print only? Both? The simplest way is to use Google Docs, convert it to a PDF and send it out digitally. However, that means that for students to participate in circulation, they have to manage and create email databases, which, yes, they can do! Of course, you can just mail it, but part of the goal is for students to interact with their school and home communities when they act as newspaper carriers and circulation managers. Photocopying the newspaper for physical distribution is the ideal method as it puts student writing right into the students' hands, and they can deliver it proudly to their batch of school and home subscribers. However, while printing the paper has costs the school may or may not want to absorb, doing the actual photocopying is also quite an act of upside down, back and forth, topsy-turviness that can take some serious practice to get right! Yes, this is an old-fashioned printed newspaper, hot off the regular copy machine! But, depending on the formatting you've chosen, it can look very authentic, though a smaller version!

While you can also absolutely get student input into the header banner design, the name of the paper, and the look, that depends on the time you have available and your group of students. For many, adding in planning time and student input over each and every decision leads to FATIGUE before the project has even started, as passions can flare over whether we go with font A or font B. Try to not get lost in the details and stick to being focused on the job of REGULARLY writing and publishing a newspaper. Not only does this add to the authenticity of the experience, but it also prevents "getting into the weeds" too much, seeking constant input and perfection when you've got regular end goals and weekly publishing deadlines that HAVE TO BE MET. Get into the story and get it out. On time.

The last bits of preparation for this project are being sure you have already frontloaded a few lessons around the process of nonfiction research and writing. Working in tandem with your librarian can help here but wait to launch the project until you've talked about how to pull details from a piece of nonfiction to write a piece. They don't have to be experts before they begin – a few sessions should do, as you can continue to weave lessons throughout the project through regular whole-group meetings and collective writing samples.

Layout and Design

Look for the most authentic opportunity you can find to start up the town newspaper. You might want to pick up a newspaper and just randomly start reading it during class time as you may or may not be surprised that many students DO NOT KNOW WHAT A NEWSPAPER IS. Open up the paper and just casually start reading it. If it has comics, all the better, as that will be of most interest to elementary-aged students. There's always one student who will wander over and wonder what you are doing. Talk to them about the newspaper. Use your powers of educational persuasion to find a natural conversational opening where you might casually mention, "That's a great idea! What if we started our OWN newspaper?" Their eyes may light up for a brief second and then quickly fade as they realize they have no idea how to actually do this. That's OK. Present it to the group as an idea anyway. If you've done other projects listed in this book, your students will already be primed to know that projects are ensconced in the idea of an imaginative neighborhood or town, and of course the town needs a newspaper!

To launch the project, talk with your class and discuss questions like:

- ♦ Is knowing what's happening around them important? Why or why not?
- ♦ Why might adults not want kids to watch the news or read newspapers?

- Should kids know about wars? Fires? Emergencies?
- What if the news only did stories on pandas and giraffes when there was a big fire in town?
- What might happen if towns had no newspapers and only heard about news from far away?
- What might happen if the news said there was an emergency and there wasn't one?
- What is the difference between fact and fiction? Fact and opinion?
- Does knowing the news help people?

Next, talk to your students about their new jobs as newspaper reporters. Oh yes, they've been hired! While you can add in an application system for students to get into certain departments if you like, it's quicker to just start mapping out the news departments on the board or a piece of paper and take volunteers. Yes, that's right – you are already jumping in, not taking a field trip first, and not comparing different types of papers with a lot of front loading. You've got a paper to publish!

Once it has been decided who is going into what department, it's time to get to work. Meet with each "department" and talk together about what they would like to research and write about. Here is a list of potential departments:

- Breaking News
- World, National, Local, and School Community News (You can split those up or join them together as one, depending on number of students)
- Facts and Opinions
- Science and Nature (You can include Weather here or move it, depending on formats)
- Arts, Culture and Entertainment (This includes music, movies, theater, book reviews, museum retrospectives, fashion, and events calendars)
- Sports (local, college, national, and world)
- Comics and Games (StoryboardThat, an online program, works well for comics)

- Data Desk
- Advertising and Art (You can combine this with Comics and Games)
- People and Places (This includes biographies, travel, restaurant recommendations, etc.)
- Business and Real Estate (Copy which businesses are "up/down" on the stock exchange, describe houses for sale, etc.)
- Jokes (We can't leave those out)
- Subscription and Circulation desk (This can be staffed on rotation by students who are finished their assignments)

It's nice to have two or three students per department "office" to keep things a bit easier to manage. That way you will have full sections instead of too many "bits and pieces". Three students writing one or two pieces for the "Science and Nature" section will likely fill up a full page, with graphics. Oh yes, the art department is an invaluable and hardworking department, as they quickly acquire backlogs of drawings for written pieces. Photograph their work and add it to the piece. You can have your writers order their own pieces from the art department to help cut down on the management. For ads, you can start with a Lost and Found ad or a "Your Ad Here" until something comes, or omit them as necessary. You can always slide a few jokes in when you have space, but the formatting of the paper is no joke!

Scaffolding
To start on a smaller and more manageable scale, commit to one paper every two weeks. Admittedly, things can get left by the wayside when the pace of the publishing takes precedence, but going so slowly that you lose momentum and the urgency of "getting the news out" can also dampen the energy of the project. The difference between publishing three newspapers in six weeks and six newspapers in six weeks can be a lot. However, to start out, go slow and take your time. Focus on student writing and the quality of their research and pieces, meeting with each

student regularly as their editor in chief. You might be surprised how many pieces your students can research and write in a short time when more time is dedicated to the process of writing.

> *We have really gotten into a 1970s newsroom feeling. Kids are practically smokin' cigarettes and asking each other "how do you spell 'according'?*
> *– Heidi commenting on the mood of her 2nd grade class during the project*

Be sure to move students around every two weeks or so to keep things fresh and ensure they are writing a variety of nonfiction topics. While the art department might not seem entirely literacy focused, researching photographs and pictures to reproduce by hand involves a lot of skill. Additionally, the art department can be responsible for creating comics, which involves storyboarding, much like graphic novels. Writers in other departments who are unsure of what to tackle could try the following tasks::

- Create or copy lists (for example, best of, most famous, landmarks, etc.).
- Draw maps (weather maps, locations of stories, etc.).
- Work on creating graphs and data (reproduce by hand or interpret).
- List market reports, data, and graphs.
- Advertise pets for adoption, real estate listings, etc.
- Create weather reports.
- Create several short pieces linked together by theme (for example, three pieces on animals)
- List sports scores, players, teams, etc.
- Write advice columns or "How-To" pieces.
- Create scientific drawings.
- Manage the spreadsheet of subscribers and help plan newspaper delivery routes.

Once your writers are humming along, it's time to get subscribers. Have the ad department start making ads to place around the school for subscribers. In any school, word of mouth travels fast and soon enough, people will be poking their heads in asking, "What's this about a paper?" You can use a Google form to start collecting email-able folks. Teach the subscription department how to read a spreadsheet and add names. Teach a few interested kids how to color code the subscribers' names and group them by area of the school for delivery routes, if doing it in person. Divvy up the list by color coded teams and deliver the paper!

Integrations

Integrating other disciplines can get tricky here, as the amount of work on one classroom teacher is, admittedly, intense. The librarian is your best friend for this project and can take some of the heavy lifting off of you in regard to research skills and resources. If you can pull in a formatter, all the better. Your technology department may be able to help you with some of this, but, fair warning: it is a lot to ask of them, as the formatting can be time consuming.

You can also charge a small fee for the newspaper and use the money to help offset the cost or to donate to a cause. That involves students keeping track of who paid and can add an additional layer of difficulty, but also adds a layer of fun – and math.

Other integrations into the newspaper are as limitless as your imagination and the amount of support, cooperation, and collaboration you have access to in your setting. The newspaper is one of the most community minded projects out there and something every school should be supporting and doing in one way or another.

Outcomes and Assessments

Writing, writing, and more writing! It is easy to assess and your students will have a portfolio of their work after the project is finished. And the outcome is that with their regular writing muscles being flexed, your students turn into much better writers!

Troubleshooting

- ♦ Leave yourself a full day to print.
- ♦ Formatting takes a while to start, but you do improve with time.

- Start with the PDF conversion as many online publishing formats are costly and have quirks which can inhibit readership.
- If you can get two or three people to help you, it helps!
- Six weeks is enough time; students will start to fatigue after about four weeks.
- Don't be afraid to tackle big topics. Students' insights are compelling to readers.
- Their spelling and writing DO NOT HAVE TO be perfect; it's OK and part of the goal of the project to show the community the authentic process of children's writing. As editor, correct enough to maintain clarity to readers, but not so much to erase the process of the writer.

Extensions

This project outline was written up as a single class project, but it can easily be applied as a whole school entity, with different grades taking up different aspects of the paper and submitting to a single editor or group of editors. Again, the difficulty is the REGULARITY with which a newspaper is published versus a magazine, journal, or other long term format showcasing student writing. Those can all be done much more easily than this endeavor, but what a month or yearlong publication misses is the controlled, chaotic excitement of a real newsroom doing real things, which inevitably emerges throughout the project.

Resources

Helpful websites to begin building your resource databases:

- Ranger Rick www.rangerrick.org
- NatGeo www.natgeokids.org
- NOAA www.noaa.gov
- StoryboardThat www.StoryboardThat.com
- epic www.getepic.com
- Links to local library references for children or your school library of resources
- Sports: local, college or professional teams as well as local school teams
- Search engines: Kiddle, Kidtopia

Council of Chief State School Offices, Common Core State Standards, US. https://learning.ccsso.org/wp-content/uploads/2022/11/ELA_Standards1.pdf

Talking Timeline

Social studies: history, research skills
 Literacy: biographical research and writing
 Math: number sense and place value, highlighting mathematicians from history
 Science: development of engineering and key inventions and inventors throughout time
 Art, Music: highlighting key figures within disciplines.

Overview
This is a project where students research and write about key people from various time periods. To present their work, students feature their research within a chronological "Talking Timeline" of people from history.

Goals
Besides the basic goals of student research, reading, and writing the biographies of important people from history, the other main goal of this project is for students to gain a more concrete sense of history by being more able to place people within the context of major events and time periods.

Time Frame/Age Group
This is a three-week project, appropriate for grades K-5.

Materials
- Research materials that include timelines and biographies
- Writing materials for the final projects
- Access to various timeline tools
- Digital resources

Preparation Time/Difficulty Level: Medium

This is a relatively easy project to achieve, as it's short term and clean cut. What makes it more complex is the number of technical and digital components that can be added, as well as the infinite number of possibilities and directions this project can extend into. Many schools already have in place some sort of day dedicated to the research and presentation of various historical figures. This project can be added onto that existing project, as the aim is for students to place those figures within historical timelines and context. The hardest part is helping students to choose people to represent and making sure you have the resources to help them write about their person. Other than that, there are the logistics of the presentation, which you can work out within your school setting as desired. Done well, this project by itself can fulfill many of the standards outlined for history by the *National Council for Social Studies* in the United States as described in the *C3 Framework for Social Studies* for children grades 5 and under. The timeline also addresses many elementary math standards for place value into the thousands.

Layout and Design

Start by asking students to think about what they know about "history". Prepare to be surprised at their answers to this simple question!

Whole Group: Explore, Sort, Categorize: (Week 1)

- Talk together a little more about their general historical knowledge.
- Move into talking about some people they know from history.
- Create lists of people.
- Sort the lists into categories. The categories can be whatever the students notice or already know about similarities between the historical figures.
- Keep researching and adding different people and expand categories to work to continuously diversify as you create collective brainstorm lists of people from "back then".

This should take a couple of days and be a joyful exploration and exercise in mind mapping as you begin to collectively gather information.
- As you deepen the exploration in the first week, it will be helpful to have a "bank" of names and people at the ready for students to explore and learn more about.
- Lists of digital resources are at the end of this project's outline.
- Work with your librarian to help you develop more wells of resources.
- Continue talking about where people are in relation to the others and start to line historical figures up chronologically. This involves a lot of math and, depending on the grade, the placing of historical figures can function as a subset project within your math periods.
- Be sure you have numerous historical figures on your brainstorm boards before suggesting to students that they begin to zero in on one to "stick with".

Independent Research and Writing: (Week 2)
Once students have made a final selection, they each work to research and write about that person. This project can serve as fulfilling numerous parts of your literacy standards in the nonfiction arena.

During this time, decide what form the timeline will take. Will it be strictly digital or an in-person format? How will you present that? Students will need to sort and designate the centuries first. Some ideas for creating timelines are:

- Digital: using a Padlet timeline or a mind map
- Physical: painters-tape lines on the floor, adding machine roll paper, signs designating centuries and decades

Final Presentation: (Week 3)
For the final project, students present their biographical research in whatever form they like. Adapt the project requirements to

suit your needs and work with students to come up with their own ideas, but some to have at the ready are:

- Standard research paper or slides presentation
- Fast facts
- Comic strips/graphic novels
- Create portraits or Vokis www.voki.com
- Paper dolls or cutouts
- Representing through costume/impersonation
- Artifacts, dioramas, or posters
- Video presentations or movies

Scaffolding
This project unfolds in a standard sequence as students:

- collectively conduct research on various people from history
- each decide on one person to focus on
- work to place that person in the context of a time period
- write up age-appropriate biographies of that person
- present their research.

To accommodate various grade levels, if done towards the latter end of the school year, kindergarten-aged children are very capable of writing basic "who, what, where, when" biographies and knowing basic facts about a person they researched.

Timeline
The timeline portion of the project can be done within developmentally appropriate guidelines, with younger students focusing on answering the question "Did they come before or after?", working to line up both people and artifacts from history in sequential order, while older children focus more closely on the specifics of place value and the planning of the timeline. Whatever the approach, ensure that older students are including details about time within their presentations by adding writing prompts, such as:

- "When was your person born? When did they die?" (K-5th)
- "List three major events that happened during your person's life." (2nd-5th)
- "List two important works of art, music, or literature that were created during your person's lifetime" (2nd-5th)
- "List two important inventions that occurred during your person's lifetime." (1st-5th) For Kindergartners, ask "Were there cars?" or "Were there books?"
- "What wars or conflicts were happening within your person's lifetime, if any?" (K-5th)
- "List three important people who died before your person was born and three people born during your lifetime." (3rd-5th) For younger grades, have them list one on either end.

The timeline presentation portion of the project can be done in numerous ways, as simple or complex as you like. A simple version would be that one class of children simply lines up in time order. Kindergartners can think about the answer to questions like, "Who comes first, George Washington or Coretta Scott King?" Or, combine with other classes and create a giant timeline. You can also do the entire project digitally and embed student projects into one large timeline, using student work and photographs. Additionally, you can create a technological timeline that focuses on the inventions of time periods and have students organize themselves sequentially around artifacts. Whatever your specific approach, it's important that part of each student's project demonstrates they have an understanding of their person's lifespan and time within history.

Integrations

While literacy and history form the foundation of this project, virtually all subjects have standards that can be fulfilled through this project. Within the timeline itself, place value is a major piece of the project as older students work together to construct digital or physical timelines. Additionally, there are numerous digital applications for students to explore and use within this project:

- Padlet to create digital timelines
- Vokis to create talking representations that can be embedded into larger constructs
- Mind mapping digital tools to help sort and categorize people
- Wakelet for collection and presentation of information
- Voicethread presentations
- StoryboardThat for creating downloadable graphic novels and comic strips.

Outcomes and Assessments

While you will have the initial assessment of the written biography or presentation from each student, it is important that within that piece of work are details related to what was happening at the time in which the person lived. Having students include and answer questions related to time periods is an essential part of the assessment of the project. Include your specific questions on a sheet and designate research periods for students to answer and explore those questions using your gathered timeline resources.

Troubleshooting

As a classroom teacher, it can be difficult juggling twenty-five different research projects with elementary-aged students. There are some alternative approaches to streamlining:

- Use premade online resources to ease the amount of management on the teacher as students can research more independently.
- Designate certain classes work within certain time guidelines so that the timeline portion of the project is streamlined (4th grade is working with people in the 18th century, while 1st grade is working on people from 1900 to 1950).
- Work in small groups and have each take an aspect of one person's life.

Ensuring Diversity

Part of the work is uncovering the stories of people hidden from history. History is about saying "hi" to new stories: "hi-stories"! For this reason, be constantly on the lookout for new, interesting people to add to your resource database. However, know that in many cases it may be difficult to uncover one individual's story, for example, who invented lacrosse, as it was developed over time and throughout North America and played by numerous Native Nations. To include it in the project, students could choose one specific Native Nation that was known to play lacrosse and research and discuss more broadly the history of that Indigenous Peoples. To ensure diversity, it may be helpful to develop choice boards comprising both periods of time and people within a spectrum of identities and ethnicities. That said, if a student is interested in researching a Black woman mathematician from the 1600s, then discussions surrounding why that may be challenging can provide enriching conversations.

One note: students and teachers should talk together about who they choose to research and represent. While some historical figures may have been instrumental in world or national events, they may not make the most appropriate selection for students to highlight. Please use your professional discretion and guidance.

Extensions

There are numerous extensions to this project and students will surely have more themselves as they work to make this project their own. One possibility is to work more closely with local libraries, organizations, and museums that are focused on histories of people, or to focus specifically on the people in the history of your town, city, or general location, or within one or two specific disciplines. Experimenting with the perimeters of the project can yield many interesting new possibilities!

Resources

- African American Heroes, National Geographic Kids https://kids.nationalgeographic.com/history/topic/african-american-heroes
- BrainPop list of historical figures https://www.brainpop.com/socialstudies/famoushistoricalfigures/

- Epic! getepic.com (Create lists of books or use existing collections.)
- Fashion History Timeline, Fashion Institute of Technology, State University of New York https://fashionhistory.fitnyc.edu/
- Heilbrunn Timeline of Art History, Metropolitan Museum of Art https://www.metmuseum.org/toah/
- Hispanic Heritage and Inventions, United States Patent and Trademark Office https://www.uspto.gov/learning-and-resources/inventors-entrepreneurs/hispanic-heritage-and-inventions
- Mathigon list of Mathematicians https://mathigon.org/timeline
- National Inventors Hall of Fame https://www.invent.org/inductees
- National Women's History Museum https://www.womenshistory.org/students-and-educators/biographies
- Timeline of African American Musicians, Carnegie Hall https://timeline.carnegiehall.org/timeline

National Council for the Social Studies, The College, Career and Civic Life (C3) Framework for Social Studies, 2010. https://www.socialstudies.org/system/files/2022/c3-framework-for-social-studies-rev0617.2.pdf

Picard, D., & Bruff, D. Digital timelines. *Vanderbilt University Center for Teaching*, 2016. https://cft.vanderbilt.edu/guides-sub-pages/digital-timelines/

The Little Library

Social studies: culture and community, history

Literacy: Integration of knowledge of literature, building vocabulary, information management, library, and media organizational skills

Overview

This is a play-based project where students organize, staff, and operate the classroom library.

Goal
The goal is for children to develop an understanding of how books are organized, counted, and sorted and to encourage a love of reading. Book clubs can easily be incorporated as part of this project.

Time Frame/Age Group
This project is appropriate for kindergarten and up and can be done in small groups that rotate into the library center throughout various periods of time or condensed within a two- or three-week focused unit.

Materials
- Classroom library of books
- Blank library cards or index cards
- Book display holders
- Pocket charts
- Librarian's desk area
- Play beeper, to "check out" (for example, an old glue gun not plugged in)
- Play phone
- Computer and/or keyboard

Preparation Time/Level of Difficulty: Easy
Depending on how your classroom library is set up, you may want to wait a few weeks to "give it over" to students working on this project, or you may want to start it right off the bat, depending on levels of need, student interest, and comfort.

First grade and older students are perfectly capable of sorting books, recording titles, and checking books out to friends in pursuit of developing a classroom library system. They will happily and joyfully involve themselves in setting it all up. You will want to wait until the end of the school year to do this with Kindergartners, as they need time to develop a deeper understanding of what a library is and the sorting and organizational skills necessary for a smooth play project experience.

Layout and Design

Basically, this is you, the teacher, wholly surrendering the classroom library over to your students. Small groups of students can work in the library during your reading time, which can add a new dynamic to literacy blocks. The great advantage to this project is that it doesn't take much additional setup, as you just need to add in a librarian's desk and checkout area to set the stage and be willing to add more props in at the request of the student librarians.

You may want to make this a rotating job where teams of students operate the library on certain days or within a set amount of time. It is important that they have some sort of structure or end goal that they can talk about and share, so be sure to meet with them to discuss their plans for their final presentation.

Scaffolding

The beauty of this project is that no matter where your class library is in terms of development, students can meet it where it is and take it to the next level. The possibilities are as limitless as within any library! Here are a few possibilities:

- Set up a "return book" bin for library visitors and a system of restocking.
- Develop a card check out system.
- Catalog books and create a spreadsheet of available or checked-out titles.
- Research favorite authors and illustrators.
- Analyze diversity representation and distributions among titles.
- Visit the school library and showcase exciting new titles to the classroom.
- Interview and work with school librarians.
- Research the history of libraries (famous libraries or different types of libraries).
- Create informational posters or accounts of how library systems work.
- Operate additional or special book clubs (in ways you surely never thought of!)

- Set up special displays or events.
- Write book reviews and recommendations for younger students or classmates.
- Give book talks.
- Develop and host book clubs.
- Create commercials for favorite books.
- Create interesting centers in the library about a setting or character of interest.
- Create virtual book bins through epic or in Padlets.

Integrations

Library and media studies is an obvious integration, but multiple subjects can be integrated as well, through books and media related to just about any subject or topic. Additionally, this is a good place for students to fluidly work with technology, as they can create databases of materials and collections of interest or importance. Additionally, creating "pop-up" resource libraries can yield interesting collaborations.

Outcomes and Assessments

The goal of the project is for students to take ownership of the library, to learn and experiment with how libraries are organized and to help them each foster a love of reading. Students should be prepared to present their system design, programs, and plans for the Library either verbally or through a written format.

If you are rotating groups, give time for them to present their work at the end of their rotation. If you have a very large class, you may want to split the project into two or three sessions to make it easier to manage so you aren't listening to presentations all year or having student systems bump up one against the other. Once groups have decided on a specific project angle, meet with them to discuss their ideas for assessment and what success would look like to them, to assess projects as needed.

Troubleshooting

This project may take a strong stomach for some used to having their classroom library "just so". Striking a balance between ensuring things don't go off the rails and allowing your students to "make it theirs" takes experience and some guts. To wade in slowly, limit it to one of your bookshelves or a smaller area and branch out as the students prove to themselves (and you!) that they are indeed capable and take pride and ownership of the space.

The trouble with making this a longer term, rotating job is that systems will be inevitably changed with each rotating group. That can work, depending on your class, but it will take significant and regular checking in and management on your end. An interesting exercise could be to ask them their plan for how they are going to organize and operate the system. With class variations, sometimes the more you stay out of things, the better. Other times, you will need to have a plan at the ready.

Extensions

Creating digital resources and directories may be something older elementary students could get into with guidance from your librarian or technology department, depending on your school policies. Other than that, students love to make slideshows and presentations and can create digital book talks, directories of talking characters, or anything they can dream up!

Resources

Some websites that may be helpful to this project are:

- getepic.com
- StorylineOnline.net
- Padlet.com (helpful to create online book databases)

Council of Chief State School Officers, Common Core Standards. https://learning.ccsso.org/wp-content/uploads/2022/11/ELA_Standards1.pdf

Expanding Circles Social Studies Projects

These last three projects are designed for students to explore civics as a concept and subject matter. These are NOT the traditional idea of "school elections" of a "school cabinet" consisting of a president, secretary, and treasurer. These projects are aimed at giving students authentic opportunities to, both playfully and seriously, participate in democratic systems.

The "expanding circles" component relates again to the slowly increasing scale and growth of the project, starting with immediate classroom circles and expanding outwards to school or community wide systems for students to be able to see how smaller systems fit into the larger picture. The following three projects can be woven together to form a full year study.

Each of these projects challenges the adults of the school community to seriously explore and contemplate the degree to which the students of the school are entitled to actual rights of citizenship within their school community. That isn't to say that schools must suddenly become models of full-blown democratic schooling, rather, these are projects that occur within guidelines and timelines that are designed to teach the process of democracy that will challenge and push the thinking of the entire school community.

> *For the things we have to learn before we can do them, we learn by doing them.*
> – *Aristotle*

The School of Citizens

Overview
This project involves the whole community exploring the idea of students as citizens of the school and the rights, procedures, freedoms, and outcomes that may arise from reframing the concept of "student" to a citizen of the school.

> *The primary purpose of social studies is to help young people develop the ability to make informed and reasoned decisions for the public good as citizens of a culturally diverse, democratic society in an interdependent world.*
> – *National Council for the Social Studies*

Goals
The goal is for students to engage in the democratic process of becoming informed, active citizens through involvement in school community clubs and organizations that help form essential operations and directionality of the school.

Time Frame/Age Group
This project can last four weeks to a full year through intermittent sessions and mini-projects for K-5th grade students. Older groups of students can be responsible for ensuring younger student's voices and projects are heard and recognized.

Materials
Material requirements will vary according to student interests.

Preparation Time/Level of Difficulty: Medium
What takes the most preparation is developing or ensuring that a school or classroom culture exists where students feel heard, able to speak up, and listened to, and where their viewpoints are respected. School culture must ensure that students are encouraged to take initiative and leadership in pursuit of their interests. This is a very fluid project that requires a lot of initiative on the part of students, so it also requires teachers to be constantly looking for opportunities to help students take action and foster leadership.

> *The aim of social studies is the promotion of civic competence—the knowledge, intellectual processes, and democratic dispositions required of students to be active and engaged participants in public life...*
> *– National Council for the Social Studies*

Layout and Design
To begin, talk together about the following:

- ♦ As members of their school community, all enrolled students are considered citizens of their school. What does that mean?

- What are some things citizens should do?
- What rights do they think citizens of a school should have?
- What obligations and responsibilities do citizens of the school have?
- How do citizens make decisions?

Continue the conversation through ongoing discussion as time and interest allow. From here, you will have to foster action groups much like starting a fire without a match, nurturing behaviors and ideas from students that can sprout into specific, actionable projects operated by students. The goal of this project is for students to see action groups as an essential part of their role as a citizen of the school. Some potential student clubs and organizations include:

- Polling and data collection groups
    - "What do students like best about their playground areas? "What are their favorite lunch selections?" "What activities would the student body like more of?", etc. Groups of students can continuously generate questions and polls and then represent the data with graphs. Repeat regularly with different topical questions and groups.
- Nature, playground, and school interior and grounds clubs
    - Groups of students can investigate how they can support the care and maintenance of school grounds and interior spaces.
- Election organizations
    - Hold voter registration drives and elections involving school issues. Election time periods can parallel your school's local, state, or federal government election time periods. When annual voting occurs, subsets of students may be in charge of organizing a voter registration drive, designing ballots, operating voting booths fairly, and counting ballots.
- DEIB group (Diversity, Equity, Inclusion, and Belonging)

- This group may focus on how students are working together, issues of fairness and equity, and ensuring representation of a diversity of perspectives, literature, and voices within the school setting and community. This group can also work on developing and refining school rules and ethics.

Scaffolding

Many, if not most, schools already have some threads of this project in place. What may not be in place, however, is the weaving of those threads together to help students make SENSE of how those existing strands fit together to form "social studies" and, specifically, civic engagement. Developing the culture and habits of mind comes before fostering action and initiatives among the students. This can be developed subtly and throughout classrooms as teachers look for opportunities for informal votes as students decide things as simple as, "Should we go outside or stay in?" for an activity or other project. Once students realize that as a citizen, they have actual RESPONSIBILITIES, be prepared for a subtle shift as students also realize that while they may be able to run down the hall, they choose not to, in order to set a good example for the younger students.

Ongoing back and forth dialogue and conversations between students and teachers forms the backbone of the project, with students offering their input, observations, and ideas as teachers lead discussions and push student thinking. Students engage in a school civic minded experience and then engage in collective reflective discussion, over and over again.

School hallway behavior is the starkest example of how schools are designed to be "instructing" children on how to be an informed citizenry in service of democratic principles and yet schools are often teaching total authoritarian compliance and adherence in practice. It's fascinating to observe schools or teachers insist that children move from place to place in straight, quiet lines. Where do you see people walking in straight, quiet lines in your community? If children were to set some rules, would one of those rules be to move from place to place silently lined up one behind the other? Would adults want to move from place to place that way? Do children have the right to decide how they would like to walk?

Integrations
The most obvious integration of this project is within teachers' and schools' own practice. As school communities go, some classes are run in a more authoritarian "government" power structure, while others are more democratic in practice. As part of educators' professional practice, it is an interesting exercise to reflect on as a school community. This isn't to say that every teacher must conduct her class as a fully open and operational democracy, but rather accept the challenge of thinking about whether children are capable of learning to be responsible without an authoritarian style of leadership and instead make choices within democratic community guidelines. As this question repeatedly permeates throughout the community, integrations and adaptations of democratic practices will naturally occur.

Outcomes and Assessments
Even without the support and constructs of the other two projects outlined within the social studies section of this chapter, this project in itself should be enough for students in grades 2-5 to accomplish and demonstrate many of the standards as outlined in the United States National Council for the Social Studies CS Framework, especially in regard to civics up to grade 5, including:

- ♦ Know some things citizens do and explain essential roles of citizens within democracies.
- ♦ Be able to talk about democratic practices vs authoritarian governing structures.
- ♦ Be able to explain why working together is important in democracies.
- ♦ Be able to talk about power structures and potential problems democracies face.

Documentation throughout the experience used in combination with students' written and verbal presentations and insights serve as assessment for this project. Be sure to work with students throughout so they are clear about the expectations for quality work.

Troubleshooting

The "looseness" of this project may be the trickiest part, as it can get lost among the busyness of school, but it only takes a few sessions of genuine conversation and contributing acts of student citizenry before the community begins to think about and view themselves as essential to the operation and direction of the school. Help ensure success by:

- making sure groups meet regularly
- assigning teacher advisors or leaders within each specific group
- keeping tasks short, achievable, and goal oriented
- rotating groups frequently
- having older grades report out their work and findings to younger grades and become leaders
- having students write short reflections and observations related to democratic practices regularly
- regularly writing down student observations and quotes from ongoing whole group conversations.

Additionally, it is important to know that kids are going to make mistakes, as they are not developmentally prepared to fully predict the consequences of their actions. While it is good for students to experience a few days or even weeks of disappointment or regret when their classmates voted against having a special "literary club day" or proposed initiative, recognize when they've had enough – when they need to be rescued – and bail them out accordingly. The point of the project is not to reenact "Lord of the Flies", but to get children thinking of themselves as part of a whole where their voices and choices actually matter.

Extensions

Working in tandem with the other two projects in this section on social studies projects, this project forms the basis for the other two, as it focuses on the rights and engagement of the school citizen. In the United States, "We the People" hold up the three branches of government. Combine it with a study of the US Constitution or other documents outlining citizens or basic human rights.

Resources
National Council for the Social Studies, The College, Career and Civic Life (C3) Framework. https://www.socialstudies.org/system/files/2022/c3-framework-for-social-studies-rev0617.2.pdf

The Right Question Institute https://rightquestion.org/what-is-the-qft/ (An organization dedicated to helping students and teachers formulate better questions as part of promoting active roles in democracy)

Government Roles and Leadership

Overview
This is a K-5 community play-based project that challenges students to seriously "play at" taking on various governmental roles within a school setting.

Goal
The goal is for elementary-aged students to be able to discuss the democratic process and the role various governmental jobs and positions play within democracies, as well as be able to discuss some of the challenges governments and democracies face.

Time Frame/Age Group
This project can last anywhere from two weeks to a full year in intermittent sessions.

Materials
The materials for this project are limited, but students will need a place to "congress" as well as writing tools.

Preparation Time/Level of Difficulty: Hard

What makes this project difficult is that the adult school community must be prepared to repeatedly ask the question, "How democratic am I, and the school, willing to be?" While teachers may come up with REAL ISSUES for students to solve, students will surely come up with plenty of topics and issues on their own and school administrators need to be prepared to engage with students seriously and genuinely on issues that are important to student citizens. This involves both teachers and administrators being WILLING to do so, so things can potentially get messy. For example, if student legislators decide to put forth a bill banning homework, the "executive branch" school administrators must be willing to veto or approve and sign the bill. It will be helpful to the process to have a number of issues school administration may be willing to yield on or negotiate at the ready and a few other issues that are more accessible for student voice and choice.

Here are some sample issues about which students can write and propose legislative bills:

- Drafting school codes of conduct and constitutions
- Procedural questions, for example, what to do with the "Lost and Found"
- Rules: for example, on the playground, "Can we go up the slide?"
- Academic choice: topics and subjects' students would like to learn more about
- Creating special days, assemblies, and celebrations
- Proposing school environmental needs bills: water quality, planting more trees, more natural play spaces around the school, etc.
- Proposing additional sports and recreation activity spaces or equipment
- Addressing community funding fairness and allocations to the school
- Input on school lunches
- Selecting social justice projects for the year or for student contributions/advocacy

As you start thinking about the possibilities for students to make more decisions in their schooling, it can become a bit overwhelming, as you start realizing how little choice and voice students actually have, as citizens of their school, in the direction of their own schooling. While this project can potentially become unwieldy and revolutionary in scale, it can also be done while maintaining respectful, ongoing dialogue between constituencies.

Layout and Design

This project is best run by a neutral party – a librarian, vice principal or support team member who can handle being in tight spots and who may need to be ready to step in and provide strong guidance and give counsel to both students and educators. Unless you are in a school setting that embraces this project wholeheartedly, to do it in K-5, you will likely have to slip it in wherever you can, outside of school classes, often needing to find a few minutes here and there to operate. The beauty of the project is that you can also scale it down to just occur within one or two classroom settings.

Basically, the school principal functions as the Executive Branch, be it Governor or President, depending on the size of your school. In the United States, Governors would work well, as students can then get the idea that classrooms are like towns and municipalities and that other schools each have their own Governor. Classroom teachers are then "Mayors" of their class towns. Modify the roles to fit the systems of your country or scale of project. Outside of the United States, modify as your government functions.

For example, to "play out" the US system of government, younger grade students can function as "Representatives", with two children rotationally selected to attend the whole school "Congress". Older students can be "Senators" and help function as leaders of the process to provide continuity between congressional sessions.

Scaffolding

START SMALL. For the first year, one or two teachers can try it within one classroom for a short amount of time, with students "congressing" about a classroom procedure or rule. It is important that it is made clear through the introduction of this project that this is a playful approach rather than a hardcore role-playing session. Perhaps more than any project listed in this guidebook, this is the one that most adults will have a hard time allowing to happen without stepping in with too much interference. That is largely why it's so difficult!

When first implementing the project within the classroom, lead by introducing a conversation and then slowly building more formal procedures into it instead of starting with the formality. This is how play thrives, as students become more assured and confident that they are allowed lots of freedom to help direct the project rather than being beholden to imposed formal rules of operations. A sample introduction may go as such:

> *So, we had a problem on the playground today and I want to hear your thoughts. A student was climbing up the slide and crashed into another student who was coming down the slide. Everyone is OK, but I'm wondering if you think we need a rule about climbing up the slide, because a lot of teachers are thinking about making one to help kids stay safe and I want to know what you think. Do you think we need a rule? Why or why not?*

Encourage students to stand up and give a reason – or three – why they think one or the other is a good idea. Help everyone learn to respect each other's opinions and voices and work to help students each see the potential downsides to their positions. After some debate, the issue can either be tabled or furthered to bill status, decided by vote. A committee can then take up formally writing up the bill and bring it back for review in your next congressional session. Once students have played at proposing and writing up several pieces of legislation, depending on their interest level, see if they can get a bill to the principal's desk after students have secured enough signatures for the bill to formally pass. It doesn't have to be perfect, it's "seriously playful".

What you will see happen is the rapid passing of many "laws" and rules that teachers and other adults may be very surprised by. That's OK. "Mayor" teachers guide the process, helping student "legislators" slow down, watching what happens during pretend congressional sessions and helping students work to become more able to see potential consequences, defend their thinking, and engage in respectful debate. As a few classes become more familiar with the democratic process, start selecting members of Congress. To start, have frequent rotations of students so everyone gets a turn. Older elementary students can eventually act as "Senators" as they gain experience and have longer terms in office than "Representatives". Laws then may be challenged by other members of the citizenry in a court of law, as outlined in the next section of this chapter.

Some authentic rules collectively written by Heidi's 2nd grade class during this project:

- *"The scooter limit is five minutes."*
- *"Two people on the big scooter, one person on the little scooter."*
- *"You have to have a scooter driver's license to drive a scooter."*
- *"No crazy sports. You can do LIGHT kicks back and forth."*
- *"Do not cut paper that is not yours."*

Over and over, adults will need to be reminded that this process doesn't have to be an exact replica of government; rather, the project acts as a proportional representation of the democratic process as time and scale allow. It's OK to have it proceed "messily" as, true to form, democracy has its fair share of that as well!

Integrations
The next project outlined in this section discusses how to integrate more voting and the electoral process as well as the role of the judicial system. Fold in talks and readings about the process of government. Writing, research, reading, and library skills are a core part of the project and are easily incorporated as students write bills and figure out how to get bills passed.

Outcomes and Assessments
Through this loose, playful reenactment, students will have gained core insights about the process of government. Even done on a very small scale and for a short amount of time, approaching

this project through a play lens has a dramatic impact on even young students' knowledge of government systems. As a final project, document the collective insights, observations, and comments of younger students. Older grade students can write about their discoveries and insights or present a session of their School Congress to parents and guests.

> *Without the citizens, the house of government would fall apart. Kids need to learn about how to be a citizen so they can work together to hold up the government.*
> *– Collective reflection from Heidi's 2nd grade class*

Troubleshooting
As passions can ignite during this project and potential issues can arise between the executive branch and the legislative, having a neutral advisor is essential. Talented executive branches (School Principals) should be able to negotiate with Congress (student citizens). The neutral party can help mitigate any problems that may arise and redirect the focus back onto procedure by ensuring bills have proper support among constituents and are properly written and voted upon. Additionally, to press even further into this project, parties involved in especially difficult situations may want to file a court case and take the issue to the next level of the process of democratic civic engagement.

Other than that, adults are the largest roadblock to this project and should commit themselves to reflection and contemplation as much as they can to allow processes to play out. Adults will inevitably try to control and dictate rather than guide, especially as things really start getting interesting. Barring safety concerns or out of bounds behaviors, it will challenge many adults to allow students to fully engage in this playful recreation as much as time and tolerance allow.

Extensions
Attend a session of your local government in process. Expand into the judicial and voting systems, as outlined in the next project.

Resources
For those needing encouragement to take on a project like this, Alfie Kohn wrote an article on "Choices for Children" here: https://www.alfiekohn.org/article/choices-children/.

The Right Question Institute https://rightquestion.org/what-is-the-qft/

In addition to eminent and essential texts such as John Dewey's *Democracy in Education*, there are multiple academic journals and schools of thought dedicated to democracy and education. The democratic process and role of schooling also form core values that are central to numerous educational organizations. Additionally, there are many models of entirely democratic schools such as the Sudbury model in the United States worth further inquiry.

Peace, Equity and Justice

Overview
This is a play-based project designed to help students learn about the Judicial Branch of government and to promote peace and equitable treatment among the student body.

Goals
The goal is for students to acquire a basic understanding of the role of the judicial system within government, acquire vocabulary, and acquire a sense of procedural and operational duties. Older grades take on leadership roles that promote peace and understanding.

Time Frame/Age Group
This project can last two to six weeks and is designed for teams of older children to work with younger students on problem-solving skills and techniques. Younger children can play the fictional court cases out through a teacher using puppets or in whole group discussions.

Materials
- Setting where a court can convene
- Gavel (playdough mallet or meat tenderizers work very well)
- Judge's robe (for example, a graduation robe)
- Desks or podiums for the lawyers
- Briefcases

Preparation Time/Level of Difficulty: Hard
This project should ideally be done after students have experienced "Math Court" and "Math Debate Teams" as outlined in the previous math section of this chapter, so that students have experience and procedural understanding of court cases. Without those scaffolded experiences, this project can still be done, but will be much less formal and more exclusively play-based.

Layout and Design
The "small circle" of this project begins with the "Math Court" sessions as previously outlined in this chapter. Once students have gained some sense of the procedures of court, the project can expand into the larger circle of all school court cases involving more complex problems and issues. These may be mathematical in nature, or they may move into more civic minded fictional cases featuring problems and issues surrounding the rules and procedures of the school and its citizenry.

The delicacy of this project is keeping things playful in nature while allowing students the opportunity to fully throw themselves into the role. This is not "Mock Trial for Kids", as those types of projects tend to be scripts for children to follow rather than driven by spontaneous play and inquiry.

The second piece of the project is promoting peaceful problem solving where teams of older elementary students work to roleplay and model respectful dialogue and disagreement. Small rotating teams of students work throughout the year on modeling solutions and problem solving for younger students. Teachers from various grade levels submit common issues and problems to the teams to address throughout the year to ensure privacy and appropriateness of issues.

Scaffolding

For court, discuss or make available the various job openings and descriptions and allow students to explore the roles and system for a while on their own without much guidance as they work together to figure out and interpret the various jobs and roles. When the time seems right, hand the bailiff a fictional conflict or problem and allow students time to see how they will solve this case using the knowledge and skills they've developed in Math Court and having interpreted the roles and jobs. Fictional problems could be:

- Court Case #244: Petunia Problems had her ring in her locker, but it wasn't there when she came back from lunch. She thought she saw James Jesse by her locker. Now Petunia is saying that James took her ring, but James says he didn't, and he is really mad. He is taking Petunia to court. How will the judge rule?
- Court Case #45: Marcus Munch was really unhappy when he saw that Gayle Gasper had cookies in her lunch, because he really likes cookies, and he never gets them in his lunch. Gayle came over and wanted to sit next to him at recess, but he didn't want to, and he stomped away. Gayle got mad that he stomped away and now she is saying that he is a bully. Marcus said, "You can't call me that" and he is taking her to court. How will the judge rule?

Let the students figure out what to do, allowing them lots of time to play and experiment with this fictional scenario. It is important that it is playful rather than directed. If you have a robust and open play culture, the cases will take on a life of their own as students own the project. They should be focused on play first and procedures second as they work to problem solve and create solutions and organically develop procedures. As the play takes hold, teachers look for opportunities to drop nuggets of information, clarification, or guidance into the play scenario. A well-placed question such as, "Who will stand up for the other person's side of this problem?" can help students begin to see that everyone needs fair representation.

Once the system is in place, one scenario feeds the other as peacemaking teams then take that problem to younger grades and model ways that it could have been solved before it got to court. Alternately, problems that come up through the peacemakers are eventually presented in court as fictional, age-appropriate problems.

Integrations
Issues surrounding inclusivity, school culture, friendship, fairness, equity, and current events are all integrated within this project. Music, art, and mindfulness practices also have roles here promoting peaceful problem solving and habits of mind. Court cases can always be math cases as well and be used to present and model court procedures. Additionally, you can use appropriate landmark cases as hypothetical cases for students to solve as well as incorporate a Bill of Rights or rights for citizens document of their own design.

Outcomes and Assessments
Ideally, addressing and highlighting common, everyday issues that arise with children helps build a school culture that is more inclusive, kind, and empathetic towards one another, while also promoting respectful dialogue and disagreement. Students can provide written and oral explanations of general court procedures along with how they would solve or rule in a hypothetical case.

Troubleshooting
It is important that this project remains playful and age appropriate for children and doesn't spiral into talk of jail, or topics that may be sensitive for students. Keep the focus more on ethical dilemmas and looking for solutions for common, everyday problems that children face within the social setting of the school.

Extensions
Once students become skilled at the play scenarios, consider modeling some cases on Zoom or Google Meet for parents, guests, and caregivers. Additionally, work to incorporate issues

of global peace and conflict as well as working to promote more global education and understanding.

Resources
John Hunter's "World Peace Game" is an excellent resource for anyone looking to incorporate more peacemaking into their curriculum. https://worldpeacegame.org/the-game/meet-john-hunter/

4

Nature and the World

Science and Movement

Philosophy and Application

These projects are intended to get children outside, moving, experimenting, and learning more about their world. We are doing children a disservice when "receiving an education" means to ignore the natural world around us, or to study faraway lands without knowing any of the plants, trees, and animals in our own backyards. Understanding and learning about the natural world is a literacy and far too many are completely lacking any vocabulary.

Children are naturally curious and learn through movement. We can sometimes minimize or dismiss developmental needs as behavioral and emotional constraints that need to be tolerated rather than embraced, educating children as we would adults, rather than listening and learning from their unique questions and leaning into their rhythms, methods, and interests. These projects aim to honor relationship building, inquiry, and the natural development of the child while promoting curiosity about the natural world.

Community Gardens

Overview
If your school does not yet have a school garden, here is your chance to get started. If you already have a garden or garden area, it may need a refresh in terms of integration into your curriculum. While there exists extensive programming, training, and system support available to teachers through grants and organizations focused on promoting school gardens, this project serves as a reminder of how valuable even a small plot of soil where children can work, dig, and plant is to the overall health and wellness of your school's program and offerings.

Goals
Students invest energy and attention into the care of the garden with the goal being to increase students' overall health and wellness along with their ability to better identify and classify numerous native plants, herbs, flowers, and vegetables, as well as helpful and harmful insects and gardening practices.

Time Frame/Age Group
The length of the project can vary from two weeks to a full year, depending on your local growing time. It is appropriate for all ages.

Materials
You don't need an elaborate or large area of land to get started – a small plot can go a long way. You can always start small and go from there. If you are short on space, you can also do a lot with container gardening. While many may tell you the importance of raised beds and extra materials, an area of the school that gets sun, that is somewhat protected, and is available will do. The most basic materials include shovels, some extra planting soil, and a source of water if you are working in an area where plants may need supplemental watering.

If you don't have much experience with gardening or growing plants, spending twenty minutes with a colleague who does can go a long way. Finding a quality mentor who can help guide you is a key part of the whole process and will make the entire project work much more smoothly.

Preparation/Level of Difficulty: Medium

The hardest part of this project may be securing permission for a space to work. The worst-case scenario is that you have just a couple of large pots in a sunny corner of your classroom. The advantage to working in the classroom is that you can start at any given point in the year. Outside has many advantages as well, the first being a chance for students to get outside of the classroom. Whatever your conditions are, a place to grow is essential. Depending on the conditions at your school and your time frame, students may even be able to help decide the location as part of the project.

The other thing to take into consideration is your growing season. If you are not planning to tend the garden over the summer or on school breaks, be sure that you are planting things that do not need supplemental watering or extra care. Time any seeding and crop rotations so that you harvest at the end of the school year and plant again within the first few weeks of school. Otherwise, you will have to work to connect with other community members who may be interested in taking over the plants and garden in the summer. Your class can engage in all of this type of planning and management as part of the project – again, depending on the time you have and your specific goals.

Layout and Design

When and how you bring students into the process can be a bit of an art. Bring them in too early, and you risk them doing too much planning and not having enough time for action. Bring them in too late, and it's not their project, it's yours. However you decide to approach it, always keep in mind the question, "What will students do in the garden next year?" This will help you not succumb to narrowing the project to a one-time garden design project and help keep you thinking about the longer-term implications of how the garden is to be integrated throughout many years.

The next thing you need to think about is how you will maintain the plants, as that may dictate your location and plant choices. Where are your water sources? If they are far away, can students safely carry water to and from the garden? Can you afford a rain barrel? Does it rain enough for you to invest in one? All these questions can be explored with students, or you can think through them yourself, depending on your approach and specific needs and time frames.

Once location has been decided, you may need to supplement the soil with a few large bags of soil from your local gardening center. Having students plan for transporting the soil from wherever it is dropped off to wherever it is going can be a fun bonus exercise, as students have to work cooperatively to safely haul the large, heavy bags to the garden location. Children often crave this kind of heavy work, and you may be surprised at who takes and shows leadership in cooperative physical tasks. Once the bags are in place, get some shovels and get to spreading and filling in the beds or containers.

One thing people do not plan enough of is providing enough time for children to simply play and work in the soil. This project can stop right here and still be effective. As the sandbox has largely disappeared from children's play experiences, many still crave and are looking for the tactile, messy type of play that is central to both social-emotional wellbeing and gross motor skill development. It is well known that gardening and working in soil benefits children with behavioral and attentional issues and this type of project can be incorporated into specific children's regular routine to help enhance their school day. Keeping an empty plot of dirt can yield lots of discussion surrounding soil types, composition, and health. Add water and work to create pottery.

Children need more time than you may think to work, experiment, dig, and enjoy the simple pleasures of good, old-fashioned dirt. Keep in mind that younger children will happily dig every day for years with no other expectation or outcome. You do not need to rush to plant.

It is important to spend a lot of time thinking about the goals and intent of your garden. Is it a food garden? Herb garden?

Native garden? All three? Is it a hodgepodge children's garden or a potential food source for the community? It is important to have a garden design with end goals in mind so that it more easily integrates into the curriculum.

Scaffolding

While younger children are enjoying the sensory experience of digging, older children may be ready for planting.

Engage them in the planning and research of what plants they want to grow. Bring in seed catalogs and go online to research plant needs and what they can purchase within a given budget. Small groups of children can work together on specific problem-solving needs of the garden, while other groups can document and research the process. Rotate the groups throughout the process so each group has a chance to experience each facet of the work. Rotations of focus could include:

- current problems and success reflections (whole group meetings)
- growth (literally plant growth) along with budget and expense reports
- watering teams
- planting, harvesting and weeding teams.
- food and sales teams (outreach and uses for plants)
- insect reports
- scientific drawings, photographs, and documentations.

Integrations

- Grow plants for the Perfume and Potion lab (mentioned in the Laboratory Project).
- Research and grow herbs and flowers with specific (and child-safe) medicinal and health benefits.
- Incorporate art, music, and storytelling into the garden experience.
- Research plant names and origins as well as the history of uses.
- Have students create Field Guides.

- Document the way the plant traveled from its area of origin to where it is now, or its prevalence or threatened status if it is native.
- Discuss why native plants are so often endangered.
- Discuss pollination, insects, and life cycles.
- Discuss rainwater and air quality.
- Discuss seeds, GMOs, yeast, and biotechnology.

Outcomes and Assessments

There can be numerous outcomes for this project depending on your specific goals and focus. On the simplest side of the spectrum, students can dig in soil and discuss and document their work, questions, thinking, and individual projects. While that may not seem much to make a project out of, you may be surprised at how much rich learning can come from something so simple. Another simple project is to track students' feelings and overall health and wellness before, during, and after working in the garden.

On the more complex side, the outcome of your garden could be that students create and market their own perfume lines or food products using ingredients grown from the community garden. You also might grow lettuce or food that is used in an annual cafe, kitchen, or restaurant (see Chapter Two: Museums, Kitchens, and Cafes). Or perhaps you focus on reporting and documenting what's growing. Whatever direction you've taken will determine your specific outcome and corresponding assessment.

For a final presentation, no matter what direction the project has taken, have students present their documentation and talk to guests about what they have been working on in the garden as a final assessment. Evidence and documentation could include drawings, final creations, written reports, weather and data tracking, jobs, and rotation schedules they've created, and student talks about invasive and native plants, different needs and uses for vegetables or herbs and a harvesting or active demonstration of a skill they've developed during the project.

Troubleshooting

The trickiest aspect of working in a community garden is that you may have a class full of kids and a small garden plot with a limited number of things to do. Do not plan on having a whole class full of children sitting quietly while one person digs the hole, and another puts a seed in. You will need to divide the class into teams with specific jobs and make sure each team gets to do each job to help prevent arguments and hurt feelings. It can be tricky to get the hang of at first as there's a lot of work to be done and many children who are extremely eager to literally get their hands dirty. Creating rotational work centers helps, as does incorporating research teams with specific instructions and assignments. Finally, if you can, create the garden in an area that is easily accessible to your classroom or a playground, that way the students can ebb and flow between both areas.

Extensions

While there are many organizations and nonprofits that work with teachers and schools, two exceptional programs that showcase how community gardens can be interwoven throughout curriculums are:

- The Edible Schoolyard Project was founded in 1995 by renowned chef Alice Waters and is the pinnacle of the school garden movement. They offer numerous resources and training opportunities as well as global resourcing and networking. https://edibleschoolyard.org
- The Princeton School Gardens Cooperative, begun by Dorothy Mullen in 2005, is an exceptional resource for anyone looking for models of how to incorporate curriculum and community gardens. https://www.psgcoop.org/

Resources

- Audubon https://www.audubon.org/native-plants
- Native Plant Trust https://www.nativeplanttrust.org/
- US Forest Service https://www.fs.usda.gov/wildflowers/Native_Plant_Materials/Native_Gardening/index.shtml

- Your local state, county or college native plant research center
- If you are purchasing seeds, be sure to conduct proper research and choose seeds that are non-GMO and won't cause harmful effects to the environment.

Ecosystem Expo

Overview
The Ecosystem Expo is a project designed for students to showcase their research skills in relation to the local natural habitat. Ideally, this project is done by different facets of the ecosystem being broken down into pieces and parceled out to different grades, so different grades focus on learning about one area. Presented all together, it not only forms a celebration of the ecosystem, but also provides a public showcasing of how different skills evolve over the span of elementary-school-aged students.

Goals
The goal is for students to research native plants and/or animals and present their findings in a vibrant exposition type of forum.

Time Frame/Age Group
The length of the project can vary from two to three weeks to a full year. It is ideally done with multiple grades but can be done within one classroom setting.

Materials
- Appropriate research materials and websites
- For presentation: animal/forest soundtracks

Preparation/Level of Difficulty: Medium
The tricky part of this project is securing coordination between grades. For that reason, setting firm deadlines and timelines is essential. Also, containing it to short term (2-3 weeks) or long time (all-year) may be helpful. If doing as a yearlong project, it is key for teachers to create a series of deadlines, projects and

documentation regularly interspersed throughout the year to ensure it is not a "yearlong project" just done in the last two weeks of the year.

Layout and Design

The umbrella design of this project is that it is a large, full-scale community showcase of the ecosystem in which students live. For city settings, this may look different and can be modified accordingly or be done as a separate project, layered upon this one. For the purposes of this project, different grades or classes may want to choose or be assigned to research:

- native plants
- native trees
- local wildlife (This can be parceled out to include separate classes or subgroups doing birds, mammals, amphibians, insects, etc.)
- weather systems and patterns within your local area
- water, soil, and features of the landscape
- how systems work together: biosphere, importance of biodiversity, ecology and energy, conservation (for the oldest grade/aged students).

The key to making this project work is workable timelines and a firm date for work to be completed. While diversifying the project among various subjects may add more complexity in terms of planning, it also helps ensure a project that contains many different aspects. Having each elementary-school-aged child showcase the process of their research, books they've read, and a nonfiction report along with corresponding visual data, scientific drawings, and artwork showcases a robust learning experience across the ages.

When all the projects are completed, the final presentation comes together to form an exposition type of forum, where parents, caregivers, and guests can explore and learn about the local ecosystem through the work of elementary school students. Dim the lights and have nature sounds playing to enhance the reality of the experience. It can be quite an exciting nighttime event!

Scaffolding

Within the classroom, juggling twenty different research projects simultaneously can be quite a trick, especially if those children are pre-readers or under seven years old, as they require much more guidance and attention. For young children, it is helpful to have them study something they can see and touch in their everyday lives. While exploring the soil, worms, and rocks may not sound interesting to adults, to children it is very interesting and offers lots of learning opportunities. This is true for trees as well, as they are large and prevalent in most areas and provide golden opportunities for robust yearlong studies. Whatever topic grade levels decide to explore, managing multiple topics can be simplified in various ways:

- Center work that incorporates hands on exploration and projects (i.e., for trees: children might use sandpaper on sticks and use the scrapings to make paper).
- Provide step-by-step forms that help organize student writing and research. For youngest learners: title, four things they wonder about, four things they know and corresponding drawings and labels. For older students: more formalized written research reports.
- Pull and organize your resources first.
- Incorporate the digital classroom – as outlined in Chapter Five of this book – to help you quickly provide individual resources.
- Work with your librarian or local librarian to front-load resources.

You can also partition the project out to small groups, designating one student to research one specific part of the topic. For example, if an older elementary class were to study "weather systems and patterns", five students can be assigned to "rain", each one taking on a specific aspect of rain: locality averages compared to larger areas, how the water cycle works, water composition and effects of pollution, and cloud formations, with everyone contributing to a section on floods or drought disasters. (As this is the most exciting part, hold no illusions that anyone will think it fair that only one student gets to do that – this is a book for elementary-aged students!) Finally, the five students can work together to create something of their own design surrounding their topic. In this way, they have each researched and written about their aspect of the topic but can also work together to create a unified project.

Incorporating questionnaires, interviews, scavenger hunts and multiple-choice type of games throughout as a part of each of the projects also lends an interactive aspect to the visitors' experience during the presentation, especially when students get to visit each other's presentations.

Integrations

It is helpful for teachers to have different and specific requirements and timelines for each part of the project. Ideally, the project reaches across subject areas and can be easily integrated into math, art, literacy, and science, given the proper planning.

- Literacy: nonfiction unit in reading, research, and writing
- Math: collecting, analyzing data, creating graphs, visual data
- Art: studying and creating related works of drawing, painting, or sculpture
- Science: enhancing student research opportunities and furthering knowledge base around their specific topic – create diagrams and scientific drawings and tie together ecological aspects
- Language: multiple languages can be incorporated through adding multilingual labels to drawings; really amp things up by including Latin for connections to scientific names.

Outcomes and Assessments

Students can be assessed on their final presentations: written report, quality of writing and research, the completeness of the project, and whatever other categories or rubrics you think necessary to enhance students' learning outcomes of the project. As this is a straight-up research project packaged as a large exposition, students can also visit each other's presentations and learn from those exhibitions. Providing visitors with activities can help encourage more active interaction and listening in service of learning about the topic. Another assessment can come from the community of visitors. What new facts did they learn? What actions might they take to help the ecosystem function better?

Troubleshooting

Coordinating between disciplines can be difficult. For this reason, setting a firm date is essential. While one teacher's timeline doesn't necessarily have to line up with another's, they are interdependent in many cases. This is where digital tools like planning Padlets come in handy to help keep everything organized and transparent without extra planning meetings or coordinated times for discussion. That is discussed more in detail in Chapter Five.

Extensions

- ♦ Bring in local organizations or nonprofits to work with students on topics or provide resources.
- ♦ Invite local politicians or local leaders to the presentation or to share about how the ecosystem affects their daily work.
- ♦ Action groups may form with specific objectives to help raise awareness about threats to the ecosystem.
- ♦ Extend into a letter writing campaign to stop harmful processes and pollutants from threatening the ecosystem.

Resources

Organizational and digital classroom resources are listed and discussed in Chapter Five of this book. Other resources you may find helpful for reference materials include:

National Geographic, NOAA, National Audubon Society Field Guides, local wildlife and native plant centers, local schools and universities and your local library.

The Laboratory

Overview
Elementary students often lack opportunities to work in "labs" and are eager to do so as they associate the "laboratory" with imaginative abstractions like mad scientists, explosions, and magical inventions. This playful lab project gives students the opportunity for open exploration, observation, and documentation. The focus is less on teaching exacting and specific scientific concepts and more on the scientific method and process of experimentation, documentation, and refinement through ongoing inquiry.

Goals
The goal is for students to work in a series of science labs where they are free to experiment in an open-ended way, work to record and document their processes, collaborate with others, and report their findings in a final written piece.

Time Frame/Age Group
This is a short-term, four-to-six-week project that can be done within many differing time structures: within short-term center rotations, ten-to-fifteen-minute small group or partner daily exercises, or whole class time periods for a set amount of time. It is appropriate for all ages of elementary students.

Materials
There are a lot of materials needed for this project, as different scientific concepts require a variety of purposeful materials. Many classrooms may already have these in place, but they may need to be repackaged and presented in a new way. Some ideas for labs are:

- Motors and Motion
- Kitchen Lab
- Fix-It and Repair Shop
- Water World
- Magnets

- Bones, X-Rays and Microscopes
- Potions and Perfumes
- Light
- Rocks

Some materials you may need to support documentation:

- Forms showing lists of materials related to each lab so students can easily record or check off what materials they worked with in the lab that day.
- "How-to" procedures tables where students can draw or write the steps of their processes.
- Notebooks for students to document and record their thinking.

Preparation/Level of Difficulty: Medium to Difficult

What makes this project difficult is juggling and assembling the vast number of materials needed. Taking time to create several bins containing materials for each lab will dramatically decrease the difficulty level. The other barrier here is the adult who may be tempted to rush in to teach, rather than to foster the process of inquiry and give it enough time to breathe and grow. It also can be a bit messy, so having a designated area and clean up routine helps!

Layout and Design

Depending on your class structure and needs, you can approach this project in many ways, keeping in mind that the point is to foster the practice of inquiry and documentation for scientific concepts. For those used to working with center structures, this will be nothing new as you may already use many of these in practice. What may be new, however, is encouraging and allowing much more freedom of how children work with the materials as well as training yourself to not assume knowledge in your students.

Assuming knowledge is the enemy of the inquiry method and is something that is so common and prevalent among teaching and learning. As teachers, we are driven to want to help by providing children with immediate and definite answers. We buy playdough for them rather than allowing children to create their own best playdough recipe through experimentation. There are practical reasons for that, of course, as it takes a long time and is a messy process. However, it is that exact experiential process that children are absolutely craving. They know creating potions and inventions takes time and they are more than willing to fail, experiment, and try again. They are eager to get their hands dirty and do real things. In the classroom environment however, this level and degree of experimentation is often fraught with practical barriers.

The aim of this lab project is to provide students with the experience and opportunity to work with materials that have no specific outcome, but rather involve the open sharing of "noticings", wonderings, trials, errors, reflections, and documentation. Introducing the routine of working in the lab area of the classroom even for fifteen minutes and then documenting the daily process can help students track their progress over time while they work on a project with a partner or within a small group.

Scaffolding

This project is not "fifteen fun science experiments to do with kids" or about giving students specific sets of instructions. It is about gathering materials that are both related and unrelated within a scientific topic and allowing children the opportunity to explore and work with those tools and materials in ways that may or may not result in anything.

The difference between this project and simply having some seashells out on the "science table" for "discovery" is that the aim is to include things in each lab kit that won't make sense or work and then to talk about why and what they noticed. Many science collection kits should already contain things that "won't work", such as fabric within a magnet kit. Go through each of your science standards and goals and try to include foils that challenge student thinking.

Magnets are a great place to start. Include plenty of non-magnetic items. Allow children plenty of time to experiment, play, and publicly share their findings. Encourage or require them to complete drawings and outlines of what they've discovered, as is necessary for your program or requirements. Approach the experimentation process less like a knowledge provider and more as someone who knows nothing and who the children are teaching. Your role is to provide materials that become the teacher, to help students document their learning, and to encourage students' recording of information and public sharing.

For a kitchen lab, begin by offering simple ingredients like small amounts of oil and water and then slowly expand into ingredients like small amounts of flour, salt, baking soda, and vinegar. They will, of course, want to first mix everything into one giant blob, which you can allow, or lead them through more methodically, as your temperament allows. The point is to try to allow them enough time and experience that they continue to work through to the other side of the excitement phase to be able to verbalize and share their discovery in a methodical way.

Potions and perfumes are a popular lab that can be easily done with eye droppers and various essential oils or herbs grown in the classroom or the school garden. It is an excellent lab to have students focus on writing down their exact moves and recipes to be able to recreate their particular potions.

Integrations

- Showcase student discoveries in weekly or regular science showcases.
- Create group documentations of student work and discoveries.
- Create lab books for individual student procedures and documentation.
- Incorporate Photographer and Documenter as assigned jobs within the project.

Outcomes and Assessments

This lab model project is intended as an inquiry experience opportunity to explore multiple different scientific concepts. The ultimate outcome is that students will be more skilled in their ability to engage in the inquiry method and become more motivated, methodical, and self-directed. It is a seed to have students begin to create their own "problem-based and project-based learning" scenarios and to be more willing to share their failures, successes, and thoughts through written reports and verbal presentations.

Additionally, students should be able to show lists of the materials they used, have documentation of their processes, and have records of their findings. Formal assessments can be based on the thoroughness of their written and verbal reports and documentations.

Troubleshooting

- ◆ Set up a lab area station that is easily cleaned and interchangeable.
- ◆ Save messy projects for when you are feeling strong and resilient.
- ◆ Students also have responsibilities within the lab to behave within the rules of the lab and to keep the area clean.
- ◆ Create forms for them to write down their ingredients or materials and provide step-by-step drawings or written accounts of how they conducted their procedures.

Extensions

Students can incorporate their inventions or discoveries into the classroom as part of the classroom culture. Showcase work at your local library or makerspace or invite guests to come see the body of work created throughout the project.

Sample Lab Form

Name:
Grade/Teacher:
Ingredients or Materials:
List of amounts:
Step by step method: (1, 2, 3, 4)
Discoveries:
Next steps:

Resources
Next Generation Science Standards https://www.nextgenscience.org/

Obstacle Courses and Workout World

Overview
Incorporating movement within your school day is a must for any elementary school teacher and setting. Using movement in conjunction with mathematical skill building and applications is a fun project to mix into your math program. Obstacle courses can be a great way to play with the practical applications of mathematical skills such as place value, decimals, clocks, time, and data collection. "Workout World" is the fictional gym where all kinds of physical activity within a classroom setting can take place, with a focus on utilizing and applying fact fluency and skip counting.

Goals
Children practice addition or multiplication fact fluency through a series of exercises in "Workout World." As a final project, students and teachers work together to create various obstacle courses with the goal of having each student improve their times to achieve their best personal records. Students work to time each other, record, organize, and represent the data.

Time Frame/Age Group
Workout World can be interspersed throughout the year; the Obstacle Course is a two-to-three-week project. The projects are appropriate for all ages of elementary students. Grades 2 and below can look at time and data as a whole class, while older grades can concentrate on individual data and timing.

Materials
- ♦ Workout World: series of stations, each with movement or exercise cards and number cards

- Obstacle Course: can be constructed in the classroom using classroom materials or done outside on a playground
- Stopwatches and timers
- Data recording materials

Preparation/Level of Difficulty: Easy

This project is perfect when you need to mix things up and get students moving. The only real preparation needed is the exercise cards, which you can easily make in a pinch. Even better, have the students create the cards by drawing the directions and poses for the specific calisthenic. You can also purchase movement cards or dots through most educational catalogs.

Layout and Design

Workout World simply folds into your math program as needed; it is not a project on its own, but it works nicely as an eventual part of the Obstacle Course, so it's a great place to start. Begin by setting up various stations where students can progress through a series of exercises and repetitions. Apply computational fluency practice tailored to your needs and ages of students. One possible method is to have a "five sets day" where every number card chosen is the number of exercises to be done, so if students draw a six card, they do five sets of six for that exercise. Other possibilities are having students roll a die for the number of sets and draw a card for the repetition number. Students should have data sheets to record their totals. For example:

- Station 1: squats (5 sets of 6)
- Station 2: jumping jacks (roll die for set number, draw card for repetition number)
- Station 3: table (draw card for how long to hold, roll die for how many sets)

The Workout World then eventually folds into the Obstacle Course project, with small teams of students designing the courses and each taking turns to proceed through the other courses. Students are then paired up or continue working in teams to record each other's times, with the goal of each student achieving their individual personal best.

It is important that the emphasis is on personal bests, as it helps diffuse competition among students and instead focuses on students supporting each other's individual best efforts. Students can be randomly assigned to other students as their personal data collector and recorder.

Scaffolding

If you have not incorporated physical movement into your educational program – not as "gym class", but as a part of your academic classroom – it is important that you start with a semi-organized system such as Workout World to help both you and your students grow accustomed to utilizing the classroom space in this way. Once everyone is comfortable, more possibilities open for students to design an obstacle course within the classroom, or, if preferred, outside on the playground.

Whether it be crawling under desks or tables, completing a series of exercises, balancing on a taped line, or progressing through a series of monkey bars and slides, small teams of students work together to design and plan a course which is then presented to the larger group as an individual challenge. Students can run each course twice and compare their data or save the data collection for a final course that would allow students more opportunities to improve their times.

Whichever approach you decide upon, each student is responsible for recording another student's time. They will need time and practice to consistently operate timers and stopwatches. Decide as a class if there are time penalties for missing a repetition or step of the course. Students are to record their assigned individual's times and organize and present the data as their final project.

Integrations

- ♦ Incorporate word games, visual puzzles or "fast facts" type of questions that need to be answered or solved into the courses.

- Work cooperatively with your physical education teacher to have students do the courses and timings in the gym and work the data aspect in the classroom.
- Rank and compare the different courses' data by difficulty and time.
- Create a collective data map and visual representations of the project.
- Invite spectators and have students present their data and team courses.

Outcomes and Assessments

Students can collect their Workout World data and results in a notebook to review their final totals. The outcome and goals for Workout World is simply practice with fact fluency and making connections between addition and multiplication while incorporating physical movement within the classroom setting.

Using timers provides students opportunities to organize course data and to present it on behalf of other students. Students can be assessed on the presentation and organization of that data as well as their group work within course design. Another hidden outcome of this project is fostering cooperation in designing the obstacle courses and having students develop camaraderie between themselves as they work to cheer each other on to achieve their personal best times.

Troubleshooting

Sometimes, students become either over-excited or fatigued, so it's important to intersperse physical sessions and planning and organizational sessions to help create intervals between the two, while always being receptive and attentive to individual students' needs. Any students who may not be able to, or wish not to, participate in the physical challenge of the Obstacle Course can always become backup timers and course referees.

Extensions

- Create courses for other classes of students.
- Combine individual scores to compete as teams.

- Use/compare/compete with a Rube Goldberg machine.
- Create tournaments and larger group and/or community participation.

Resources

Sample Workout World form

| Station 1: | Reps: | Sets: | Total: |
| Station 2: | Reps: | Sets: | Total: |

Sample Obstacle Course timesheet

Course number/name:
Design elements:
Time 1:
Time 2:
Best time:

Number of courses completed:
Best time overall:

Walk 'n' Talk Trail

Author's Note: The Walk 'n' Talk Trail began as a culminating presentation project for a yearlong study on trees when I taught with BA Cagney. Students took their parents on a walk along the nature trail at our school and pointed out trees they could identify along the way. The project is modified here to suit a wider variety of environments, skills, and conditions.

Overview
The "Walk 'n' Talk Trail" is a frequent and regular walk where "noticings" are pointed out and eventually mapped, discussed, researched, and finally presented by students taking their guests

on the walk and talking with them about what they have learned and discovered. This is a great project to start with if you are new to the inquiry method and want to gain experience and practice, as it's very open ended.

Goals

The goal is to spend relaxed time with students, getting to know one another and noticing things along the way. The goal is to develop inquiry skills, whether that be within the surroundings, or more socially-emotionally. Students document the "noticings" and share them through a final presentation where they "Walk 'n' Talk" with a guest adult, pointing out what they've observed and learned about along the way.

Time Frame/Age Group

The time frame can vary from two or three weeks to a full year length project, depending on needs. It is appropriate for all elementary aged students. The actual walks can vary in time from short (10 minutes) to longer (30 minutes) depending on your setting and situation.

Materials

It is not a "material", but something you'll need for this project is a regular, safe route to walk as a group. It might sound strange to suggest taking a stroll through the inside of your school, but you might be surprised at how striking the difference is when your goal is to "stroll and notice" rather than to walk in a straight line, be quiet, and get from place to place as fast as possible without running. Casually strolling through your school (*not in a line!*) with your class on a regular basis can lead you to all kinds of adventures when you approach it with the goals of inquiry and exploration. Make exploring the grounds of your school part of the walk as well and see what topics come up through regular visits, inquiry, and "noticings".

Eventually, you may like to incorporate more features:

- ♦ Blueprints and drawings of the school and grounds
- ♦ Paper to make large maps
- ♦ Appropriate research materials
- ♦ Field Guides created by students.

Preparation/Level of Difficulty: Easy

While this project is easy, it could go in a hundred different directions. The simplicity of this project can be deceiving. Encouraging students to look around, wonder, research, and learn about their immediate surroundings could lead to all kinds of possible outcomes and, depending on your surroundings, the outcomes will vary greatly. Some schools set within forested campuses might notice, observe, research, and learn to identify trees and plants and how they change throughout the seasons, while other schools set in more urban spaces might focus more on researching people and their jobs, the architecture or history of the school, or how various systems work within the school. Still, others may notice that something is missing from their school environment and devise plans to create something new.

Depending on your school climate, the trickiest part of the project could be securing permission for you and your class to freely roam about the hallways and school grounds. You may need to explain the process and scope of the project to your administration. Invite them to join you!

Layout and Design

The point of this project is to take regular, ongoing walks and see what they notice and wonder about along the way. Notice and observe changes and become more familiar with the environment through those changes and observations. Maybe it even becomes a little boring. That's OK. It's good, even. Talk along the way with your class. Keep it casual. Get to know each other. That could be the project. However it evolves, this project begins by taking regular walks for a portion of your time together. Walk, talk casually together, and just notice things, or don't, then, if you want, come back to class, and share what you noticed. It's also OK to not share and just let it be an experience of its own. This is a no-pressure project!

Scaffolding

Eventually, through the experience of regular walking, you and your students will have developed a "Walk 'n' Talk" rapport, where the kids have freed themselves up from any "extremes of feeling" like being super excited and jumpy or, at the other end of the spectrum, a bit defiant and resistant to the open-endedness of the project. After doing this about three times, you will literally, as a class, hit a stride. That is the sweet spot, as now students feel more relaxed and comfortable.

On your first walk together, you might feel a little frantic and think, "What are we doing?!" That's OK. Keep going. The worst outcome is that you get to know your students a bit better. On that first walk though, think about something YOU notice and how it could serve as a back-up project. Meanwhile, take in your students' "noticings" and think about how those could evolve into projects.

Your second walk is where you really begin to foster more inquiry among your students. Help them make connections or comparisons between what they noticed last time and this time. Make open-ended observations together. Chat about current events, talk to people around the school and, yes, it's more than fine to linger by the playground for a few extra minutes of play time. What do you notice while they are playing?

The third walk is where they will be excited to go (especially if you stop by the playground!), but it's more than that, as they now trust you on this walk. They know you aren't going to grill them, they aren't going to get in trouble for talking or not being in a line, but rather, you are walking together, as a cohesive group. It's the place where you can all truly begin to open up to the process of inquiry. After the third walk is when you begin to formalize the project.

Integrations

While you can insert many different specific academic practices and goals within the walk, one that stands out for you to keep in your back pocket in case nothing else comes up is a measuring, research, and mapping project that involves working to create accurate maps of the route you take. If you are doing this as a yearlong project, divide the project into many parts, allowing time to focus on the entire project piece by piece.

Start by researching and writing about the architecture and history of the school, then in the next few weeks, work to write up a report on the identification of all the trees, plants, and birds you've observed and identified on the school grounds.

As you continue to walk throughout the year, you will naturally develop stops along the way and can develop new lines of inquiry and research based on each of those stops. As you progress, find achievable projects that target skills in art, science, literacy, social studies, and math and incorporate them into the scope of the project. The key is to focus on one achievable thing for a few weeks, report and document your findings, and move onto the next area. In this way, as you progress, through a 10-minute walk each week and a few research and documentation periods, you will have a large body of work to present at the end of the year.

Outcomes and Assessments

Finally, have students create an accurate map of the entire walk. Each facet of the walk should feature findings, research, questions, observations, and both collective and individual documentation and writing. Students then take a guest of their choosing on the walk and they can talk together about the process, with students pointing out various things of interest along the way. Present the final collection to guests. Students can be assessed on the project through their written documentation and findings during the walk and final presentation.

You may also want to chat with students individually about things that come up during the walk. Walking together has a way of opening new doors to relationships between students and between teacher and students. Social-emotional goals should not be ignored as a vital part of this process and could even be the focus of the project. Those behaviors will teach you a lot about your students and provide you with an opportunity to know them in a different way.

Troubleshooting

The worst-case scenario for this project is that you take one or two walks together, get onto something else and the project is abandoned. That's OK! Try another year with a different group. However, you may be surprised at what persistence, inquiry, observation, and consistency can yield.

Another thing that may go wrong is fostering enough inquiry to get a project going. It's not easy but keep asking open-ended questions to keep them probing, researching, and wondering. Inquiry as an educational method goes unused so often; it may take a while for students to get used to the open-ended nature and process.

Remember to stay on school grounds unless you have secured permission slips for each of your students in accordance with your school's policies and procedures.

Finally, to circle back to a potentially hesitant administration, providing them with an outline of the project and your specific goals may help loosen them up. And do invite them along once you've established a solid "Walk 'n' Talk" routine!

Extensions

Extensions of the project can stretch and evolve as far as you can go! Walking the neighborhood and furthering the boundaries of the walk could yield interesting results, as could inviting regular guests to come along with you. Invite them to see what they notice or wonder about. Talking about, thinking, and reflecting on your school and its grounds and surroundings can yield unending potential, with the best being the opportunity to get to know your students in a new way.

Resources and References

Refer to Chapter One on the inquiry method for more specific references on how to foster lines of inquiry as well as resource lists pertaining to inquiry

5

Working Together in the Digital World

Philosophy and Application

Being an elementary school teacher means you are managing a team of twenty-five children while simultaneously juggling four different areas of academic content delivery while also differentiating for everyone within each subject. The beauty of being an elementary school teacher is that because you are immersed in so many subjects and concepts, you can find connections and create, across the board, learning experiences and projects that enhance learning around all subject areas. As elementary school teachers have yet to be siloed and sorted into academic areas, there is more freedom for teachers to foster connections and create cohesive curriculums.

Most of the time teachers are frantically working to stay one step ahead of the game. The rapid pace and demands of the modern classroom often make it difficult for teachers to have enough time or energy to think about how and where technology fits into their program. The global pandemic of 2020 pressed schools and teachers into providing a fully remote educational experience with little to no notice or preparation as schools basically transitioned overnight into fully remote operations.

While some teachers were given strict parameters to work within, others were allowed lots of freedom in choosing how to deliver their programs. The methods varied from digital worksheets to more conversational Zoom meetings to video delivery of lessons and everything in between. Too many programs became skill and drill type of exercises that led to drab, remote learning experiences. Incredibly taxing on both students and teachers, many of the digital delivery models then evaporated from the elementary school setting once schools resumed in person as everyone began to relax and recover from the traumas brought on by the pandemic. Teaching during the pandemic, many digital delivery methods reached their endpoint as they became unsustainable and impractical.

> *Finally, one day after taking 40 minutes to try to explain simultaneously to both an online and in person class of good-as-gold, capable and eager 7-year-olds how to 1.) access and 2.) fill in a PDF, I was done. Goodbye practice worksheets converted to PDF's or any of the 45 other possible delivery methods. Even IF we all got better at it, teaching students concurrently (in person and remotely at the same time) triple killed using worksheets as practice because having to create or find the practice worksheet in the first place, photocopy it, and deliver it remotely to students to use online for a mere fifteen minutes became too much to sustain. After multiple earnest attempts, I decided I needed a new way forward.*
> *– Heidi*

While many schools support technology by having teachers make goals for integration and by providing teachers with support to adapt to new tools and technologies, as a teacher it can often feel as if it is all "technology spaghetti" being thrown at the wall to see what sticks. Programs are often presented as shiny single pieces of the puzzle rather than talked about as fitting together as part of the scaffolding of your year of constructing learning. Look up several educational tools online and very often they will tell you how to buy it but provide you with little to no information on what it ACTUALLY IS, as if you are supposed to know by telepathy. Teachers, just like learners, need both time and experience to be able to synthesize and collect information, to make sense of whatever new product or technique comes into the mix and to be thoughtful and intentional about creating and delivering the student experience. This is one of the many complex reasons why so many programs end up failing or falling short when it comes to implementation within classrooms.

For all of the difficulties and challenges, embedding technology into the elementary school program can offer flexible, fun, challenging, and differentiated instruction full of vibrant and varied learning opportunities. As with any elementary classroom setting, the design and construction of the physical setting is paramount and in the digital world it is no different. An approachable interface is an essential and overlooked piece to offering young students accessible digital platforms.

Navigating Technology is Literacy

We are now firmly ensconced in a digital era where it would be extremely difficult for the average person to live without using some form of technology. To be literate in today's world means to be independent and fluent with using technology. Students need to be using today's tools to help them develop skill sets that will serve them in their future lives. While we can – and should – teach students to be able to locate and find physical books in a library, students also need to be able to safely navigate and build literacy around today's technologies. In the elementary school setting, it is not uncommon for computers to still be reserved for special project times rather than fully integrated into classrooms as foundational practice to teaching and learning. While young students need to work with hands-on materials and strengthen skills through the physical act of writing and drawing, they also need to become literate and savvy navigators of technology. We want to keep kids safe, but by not allowing them to use or learn to navigate the internet in school, we leave them wholly unschooled in the primary language of the 21st century.

While one primary reason for technology not playing as huge a role in the elementary classroom may be that young students need to touch, see, and do, another reason is that it can be difficult to make sense of how all of the individual pieces of technology fit together cohesively. While there are many applications and programs that provide exceptional programs and content, new features and programs can be thrown at teachers so fast and frequently that sorting it all into a narrative to help students make sense of the tools can be daunting. However, much like the physical materials within a classroom, using digital materials offers students a wide variety of tools and opportunities for learning.

The Digital Classroom

It is impossible for one educational platform to deliver everything. Admitting and realizing that may take some time to sink in for some, but it's a very important thing to realize. Just as one book cannot possibly contain all the information, lessons, and topics for the classroom, neither can one program. While some may want a one size fits all approach, trying to be everything to everyone will always result in watered down content. Thankfully, there is a large and rich variety of online content out there to offer children and schools. Even without adding anything new to the mix, almost every teacher can name three or four different online access points already in use as part of her regular school routine.

Managing the juggling act of online content delivery has largely been done through having students navigate through Google Classroom. However, that system quickly breaks down when working with younger students as pre-readers struggle to make sense of the rather adult oriented interface of Google Classroom. Seesaw is a platform for younger children that is an effective documentation tool, but not necessarily a robust content delivery method. Teachers and students need to use and access a wide variety of tools, rather than one system that "does it all." Additionally, teachers need to be able to make changes and customize the classroom environment for their students quickly, frequently and easily. Enter the solution of creating a digital classroom.

User friendly and attractive, the digital classroom is approachable and appealing to children. The digital classroom gives children a visual, representational, and friendly "map" for how to make sense of digital content. Created through simple presentation slides, it is an easy, inexpensive, and accessible method for teachers to create and customize a digital classroom. While many in education may turn up their noses at the simplicity of using Google Slides or a PowerPoint to deliver content to students, it is, in practice, a remarkably simple and incredibly effective way to deliver vast amounts of educational content to children. The digital classroom provides a pictorial narrative to help children navigate multiple platforms and tools and to help them build memory, understanding, fluency, curiosity, agency, and sense-making surrounding technology and digital platforms.

In online searches, the closest thing to seeing an example of a "digital classroom" is the "Bitmoji classroom", however, they are different things. For those unfamiliar with Bitmoji, it is a digital cartoon representation of a person. When you search "Bitmoji classroom" most every example is largely focused on classroom decoration and a cute cartoon teacher (the Bitmoji). Some feature a few online books and are generally filled with motivational posters on the wall and cute flags. There are numerous YouTube tutorials on how to create one.

Get rid of the decorations, the Bitmoji cartoon teacher, and the distractions, however, and you have a viable template for making something very accessible and exciting for kids to navigate. Once the distractions and decorations are gone, the classroom starts taking shape. Imported images become portals and are used to create a "real-looking" simulation slide of a classroom. Form follows function and as websites and platforms are needed, new portal images are integrated into the classroom scene. It makes planning easy, as teachers can front-load the classroom with options and have children explore them one by one. The digital classroom quickly becomes a magical door to a new, seamless flow of learning and teaching.

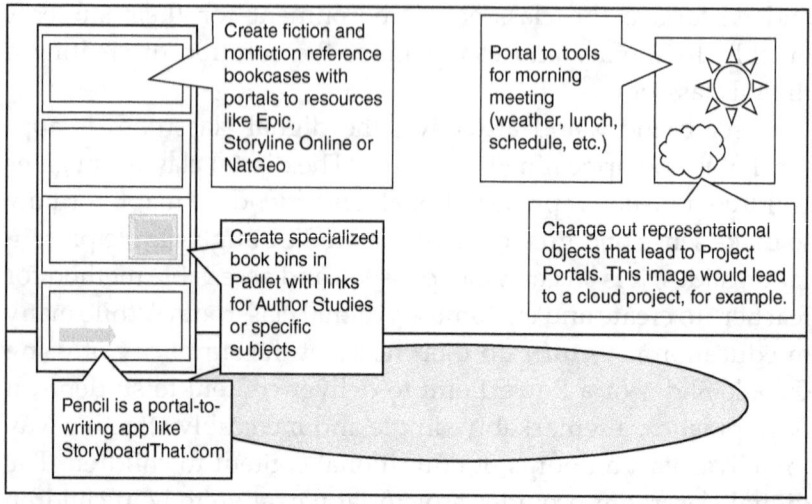

FIGURE 5.1
"Blueprint for a basic digital classroom"

After the kids' own rave reviews along with observations of their extremely high engagement levels and the ease of delivering content, I knew I was on the right track. As the work progressed, I added more and more slides into the classroom, creating specialized math and literacy rooms. To further the virtual experience, I started to use photographs of the actual school entrance and placed images hyperlinked to relevant interactive web portals all along the way. For example, one slide featured a photograph of a common area where children worked with actual tactile blocks in real life. Students could click an image of blocks superimposed onto the photograph that hyperlinked to a website where they could explore digital block building.

– Heidi

Blended Models

Moving back and forth between digital and physical models provides children with time for hands-on experiences with manipulatives, while also helping shape and drive mathematical concepts from exploration to more direct "noticings" using digital tools. For example, during a geometry unit, students work back and forth between creating 3D digital simulations and then work to replicate those structures using hands-on manipulatives and vice versa. Concepts are solidified by repeating them with both digital and physical manipulatives. Using digital resources combined with manipulatives proved invaluable at helping guide children more towards noticing more mathematical concepts.

Some other methods to use in this blended fashion:

- Enhance your daily morning meeting, where you convene with your class to discuss the daily schedule and share news from the class. Share weather routines by looking at and discussing satellite imagery from the National Weather Service.
- Students have open access to lunch menus, daily schedules, and school calendars and can independently navigate as needed.
- Students can freely work on collective projects at their own pace. Collective projects can be digital or in person, co-creating maps, playing tic tac toe or working together to create presentations.
- One of the most helpful aspects of the digital classroom is the ability to assemble and distribute resources quickly. For example, if students are each studying a specific kind of tree, you can quickly provide links to online resources to that type of tree. While there are many physical books on trees, there are also helpful – and often more precise – informative web resources right at your fingertips. Front load them onto a slide and it frees you up to work with students 1:1 or in small groups.
- Children can explore physical books as well as digital books and audio stories.
- Using origami videos to follow folding steps.

While none of these techniques alone seem revolutionary, collectively teaching and learning this way fundamentally changes the pace of working together in the classroom setting, largely becoming a much more fluid process. Lessons, assignments, and projects are interspersed throughout with lots of time and space for exploration.

Digital Classroom Design At a Glance

- Eliminate the Bitmoji character so students visualize themselves in their classroom.
- When setting up the digital classroom, never include any unnecessary decoration. Make sure every item serves as a portal to somewhere new.
- Use high quality websites and programs that are relevant to the object "portal" image (for example, a book leads to StorylineOnline.net and a whiteboard image hyperlinks to Google Jamboard or another online whiteboard resource.)
- This kind of controlled exploration of educational websites lends itself to regular and ongoing lessons about internet safety as it embeds a standard of safe practices for using technology within the culture of the classroom.
- Use additional slides to create "rooms" focused on various academic subjects and special events.
- Incorporate photographs of your actual setting when possible and add object portals on top of those. For example, use a photograph of the outside of the school and add an image of a school bus, which serves as a portal to another Google Slides presentation "field trip."
- Create an entryway, cubby and/or common area to further the digital experience. Use those as portals to essential information and for individual storage.
- Virtual cubbies or lockers can be used to house children's individual work portfolios, similar to real-life classrooms.
- While it takes a bit of practice to develop the cut/paste/insert/crop technical skills, with practice it becomes second nature. You can also create and share templates with other teachers to make it much easier and to create networks of portals and resource wormholes.

Creating a basic digital classroom setup takes about two or three hours, with the whole digital experience in full bloom in about three months. The time investment upfront pays dividends

Working Together in the Digital World ◆ 195

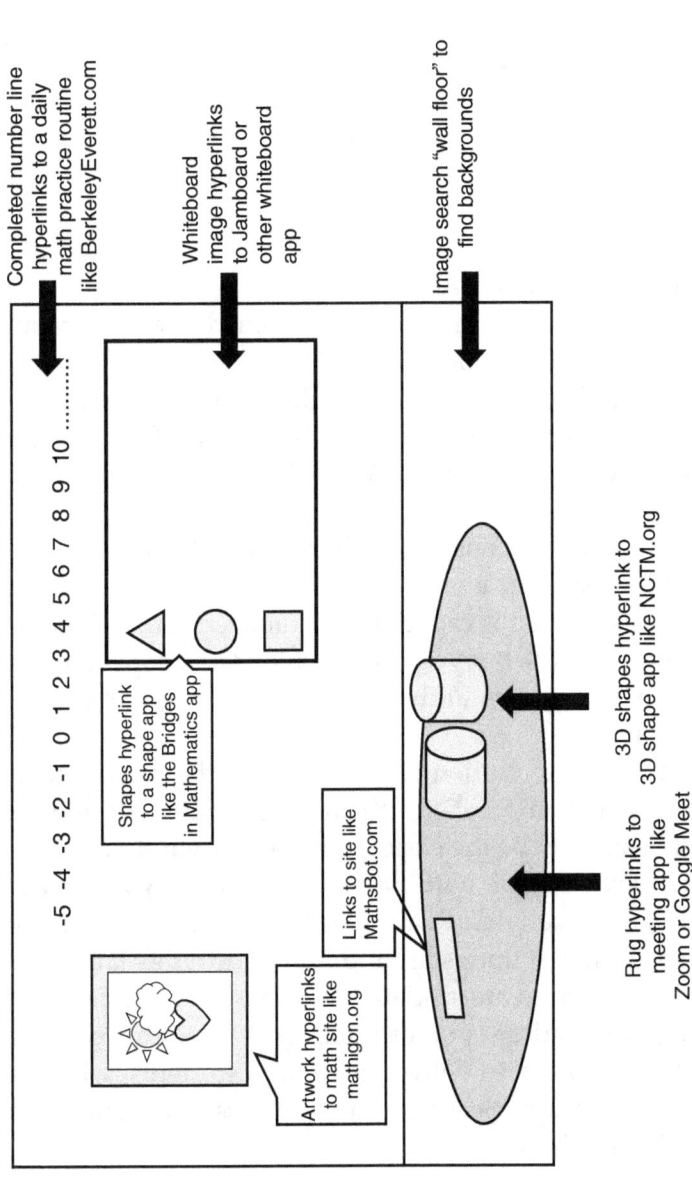

FIGURE 5.2
"Blueprint for a basic digital math classroom."

Note: The blueprint digital classroom images provided here are basic representations done through drawings to avoid the complications of inadvertently reprinting any images protected by copyright. In your own searches for images when making your digital classroom, be sure to only include images that can be used for educational purposes and have the appropriate licenses for fair use.

down the road. In class, take your time to allow for lots of ebb and flow between the digital content and traditional physical objects (paper, books, manipulatives), keeping in mind the digital classroom is not intended to replace pencil and paper or manipulatives, but rather to enhance your overall program. Once you have the basic design and implementation down, you can begin to add in some very interesting applications that have some exciting possibilities as we will see later in this chapter.

How To Implement in K-5 Classrooms

Once you have taken the time to create your digital classroom and have shared it with your class, it's time to teach students how to use it and navigate it. Much like an actual classroom, there's no need to have everything finished and perfect. It's best to start small and basic with a few core links you will use all year.

- You can view and use an early childhood version of the digital classroom already made for you at Kinderchat.org. This version is especially customized for the kindergarten age level, but you can download and copy it to use to create your own and easily adapt it to suit your own grade level.
- For delivery to students, the beauty of the presentation slide is that in a pinch, it can be delivered through a PDF. This may be the easiest method for young children who may struggle with navigating technology. Keep in mind, however, that PDFs won't update once you share them. To move things around and add things later, you will have to create updated versions. For students in first grade and up, you can deliver it through whatever method you use to deliver content to students, whether that be through Seesaw, Google Classroom, email, or another method.

Once you've delivered the classroom to students and their computers, encourage children to look around and start clicking the images. Just that can be interesting, as some children actually need help initiating clicking, as they may be hesitant to make a mistake. It doesn't take long, however, for someone to find something fun and everyone wants to know "how to get there." Sit back a bit and watch what they gravitate towards. Notice how quickly the students naturally start networking with one another, working in tandem to discover the next best thing. Your class will get eerily quiet for a while and then suddenly erupt into high energy chatting and movement. Allow that spirit to bloom and breathe. Fostering the idea of network is important and you will need to actively create an atmosphere of sharing as one student who knows how to do something can teach another. In the literacy of technology, networking is a basic skill. This is one of the most important aspects of the entire concept, as using technology should be INTERACTIVE and SOCIAL. For too many, this alone is, sadly, a revolutionary concept and many may need to reread this paragraph several times to begin to understand how the use of the digital classroom fundamentally changes classroom culture.

Heidi's Tech Tips:
1. *Don't panic.*
2. *Try stuff.*
3. *Help each other.*

To begin:
- Students get access to the template and bookmark it for independent and frequent use.
- Start by modeling "looking behind" each image one at a time and talking about what's there. Spend time talking about the weather images from the NOAA.gov website as a group at your morning meeting. Use online math materials for group discussions or to play collective games and then have students explore that tool independently.
- Create book bins using Epic and Padlet and link them to relevant objects. For example, an image of a bird or binoculars links to a collection of books about birds or birdwatching. Use these in tandem with read-alouds and independent reading with physical books.

Next Steps:
- Children continue exploring tool by tool. "Now we are going to explore the painting. Let's see how this portal works." Allow for a balance between exploration, networking, public sharing of discoveries, and task/skill-based assignments.
- Students have the option to explore the digital classroom during free time.
- Begin to integrate online math manipulatives with physical manipulatives using one to inform the other through ongoing conversation and public sharing of the math they've discovered with each, and with using both together.
- Work to have students create and document how they solved a math problem using digital materials. You can also include photographs of how they solved it using manipulatives or by using written methods.
- Begin to incorporate task-based assignments and projects. "Using digital tools, demonstrate some ways you can solve 325 + 238." For younger students, have them first try using hands-on manipulatives, document that, and then have them try it again using digital tools.
- Begin to build digital portfolios through class collective and individual work samples.

Full integration:
- Assignments and lessons freely flow between using physial materials and digital.
- Students work to independently document their work online through digital portfolios.
- The classroom atmosphere is networked and cooperative. Once children learn how to do something new, they become consultants and teachers for others.
- New projects and assignments are delivered by new portals appearing and students noticing and discovering. Regular conversations take place among students and teachers about what was noticed or discovered throughout the day.

♦ Students demonstrate fluency by navigating fluidly and independently through the classroom, following a series and sequence of directions, independently completing assignments, creating documentation of their work, and uploading work to their portfolios.

Showcasing Student Projects

On your way towards creating individual digital portfolios, a good way to begin is collective class projects. It can take some doing at first – not only the mechanics of the uploading and organization, but also the process of selecting pieces for a project. Documenting a sample of each child's work and presenting them collectively can serve as a powerful reflection of the age and ability of elementary school students. It also serves as a critical piece of documentation about how a project is progressing or unfolding. Much like a bulletin board or hallway display, this allows children's work to be shown and showcased. Presenting the work digitally through Google Slides or another presentation format allows it to be delivered through a PDF and shared to children's families and caregivers easily and attractively.

When planning units of study and projects, it is important to plan to set aside time for documentation. You will need to decide what pieces of work you want to use and how they will fit together to form a cohesive narrative. Do not leave any of this to chance; scheduling time for assembling collective projects is essential. This process must be purposeful and planned to ensure it occurs, otherwise the school day becomes eaten up with the daily demands. Students can, and should, also be a part of this process, selecting which pieces of work they would like to present. Aim to complete at least two collective project examples for the year. It will be helpful to have those samples in place when beginning to create each child's own digital portfolio.

Building Digital Portfolios

Many folks will rightly head for the hills when they hear "portfolio" as, without the proper planning, it can be a messy and cumbersome undertaking. Leaving portfolio curation to happenstance or chance is a recipe for disaster. Work samples must be planned and regularly collected to ensure the content is a true representation of the child's work on projects throughout the year.

The great part of having children work in the digital classroom is that as their fluency increases, by the middle of second grade they can construct, download, and upload their own digital work samples completely independently. It's important to scaffold in those processes slowly, as you are teaching the tools of the digital classroom.

> *Having my second-grade students create a math portfolio is a particularly effective way for the children to share their learning. Students create their own math portfolios that showcase a series of assigned problems and skills in combination with their own individual math wonderings and independent projects. We then invite teachers and parents to a Google Meet session where students independently present their work.*
>
> *– Heidi*

Having students present their math portfolio work to their parents and other members of the school community serves as a kind of "defense" where the children discuss, share, and prove their logical and mathematical thinking. Refer to Chapter Three of this book where "Math Teams" and fostering yearlong mathematical conversations are discussed in more detail. As the student has been practicing this type of "math talk" all year long, they are comfortable talking and presenting their work, albeit a bit nervous! It's a wonderful opportunity for them to showcase their work and it serves as a final project assessment and celebration of their hard work.

Special Events and Integrations

Slides created for special events are easy and quick to insert into the regular digital classroom via object portals inserted into the room. See who notices and how long it takes them to discover something new in the digital classroom. Holidays, special topics, new units, and projects can pop up and appear with assignments,

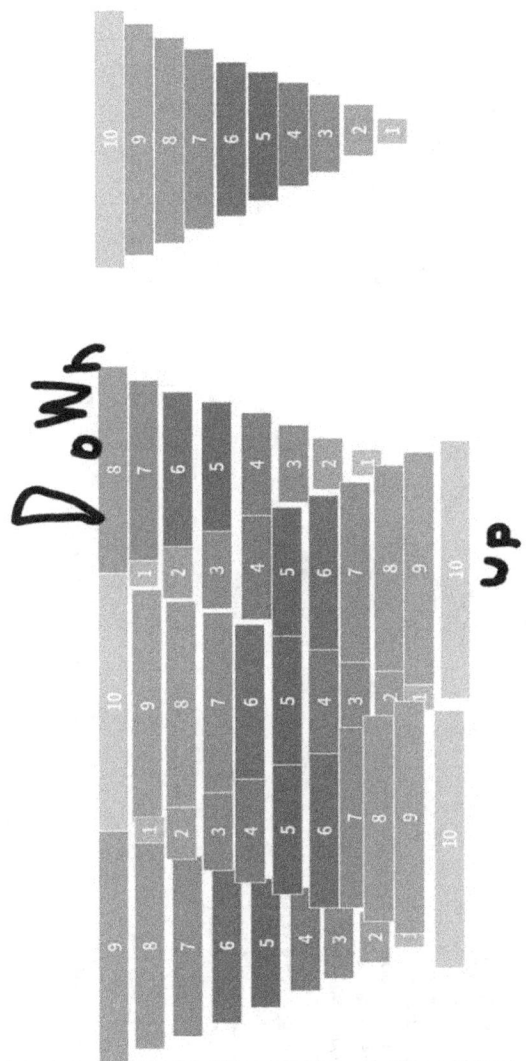

FIGURE 5.3
Charlotte J 2021; image created using the free virtual manipulatives at Polypad.org, used with permission.

This is a 3d cube

A 3d cube has 6 faces. The proof is if you have 6 squares and you put them together you make a cube. A cube is not the same as a squuare. One of the reasons is a cube has 6 faces 8 vertices and 12 edges. A square has 4 faces edges and vertices.

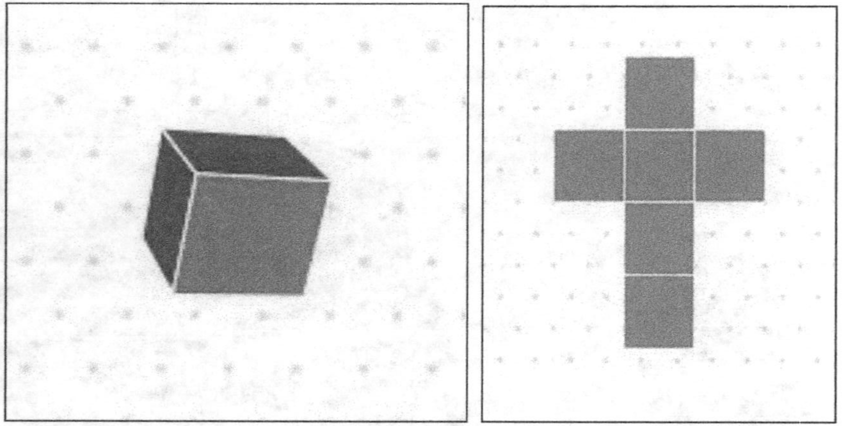

Charlotte T 2022

Image created using the free virtual manipulatives at Polypad.org.

FIGURE 5.4
Charlotte T 2022: image of 3D cube, used with permission.

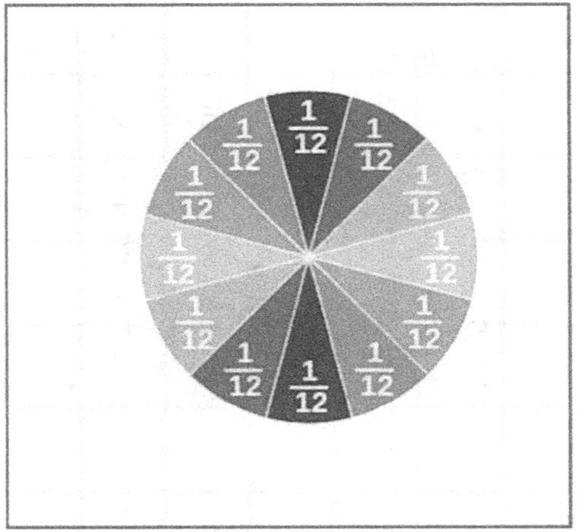

Red means january. Orange means february. Yellow means march. Green means april. Blue means may. Purple means june.

If your birthday is one of theas months just count 6 ones after it and you will get your half birthday.

If your birthday is in January your half birthday is july. If your birthday is in february your half birthday is august. If your birthday is in march your half birthday is september. If your birthday Is in april your half birthday is october. If your birthday is in may your half birthday is november. If your birthday is in june your half birthday is december. If your birthday is in july your half birthday is january. If your birthday is in august your half birthday is february. If your birthday is in september your half birthday is march. If your birthday is in october your half birthday is april. If your birthday is in november your half birthday is may. If your birthday is in december your half birthday is june.

Charlotte T 2022

Image created using the free virtual manipulatives at Polypad.org.

FIGURE 5.5

Charlotte T 2022; image of a circle divided into 12ths to explain half birthdays, used with permission.

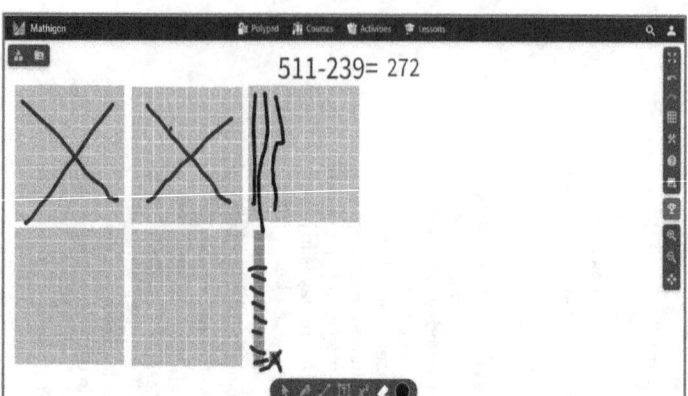

Tory 2022 *Image created using the free virtual manipulatives at Polypad.org*

FIGURE 5.6
Tory 2022 image showing a 3-digit addition problem using the free virtual manipulatives at Polypad.org, used with permission.

videos, books, or sites of interest. Creating the slides can take some time and practice, but once you have them it is easy to keep them in a folder and tweak and customize them a bit more each year.

Incorporating video games like adventure and maze games can also become a part of class culture through the digital classroom as children work together to discover new avenues and solutions for games. Video games have been shown to improve cognitive performance and enhance memory (Bediou et al. 2018) and can be used and accessed by children during free times, similar to any other learning tool available in the classroom.

Additionally, you can create slides for enhancing curricular integrations like art and music and specialized content for dual language learners. While they won't be equal to a class and a teacher, they can supplement and serve as a substitute in a pinch, as well as provide children more time, practice, and daily access to music, art, and global perspectives in education.

Large-Scale Applications

One thing about education, and progress in general, is that people are always pushing for the next big thing when they've left some good, basic ideas behind without really thinking about them. Everyone is rushing into AI, but in practice, many folks are just starting to use Google Forms, which have been around for over twelve years. Technology and education are often the story of the tortoise and the hare. Plenty of money goes into pushing the boundaries but often doesn't allow enough input, time, practice, and application regarding the functionality within the real classroom setting.

Too often, children are being "educated with technology" by simply progressing through customized mouse mazes of online learning assignments, often with very little choice or ability to make decisions, guide their own learning or work collaboratively with peers. The digital classroom offers learners all of these, as well as a unique and unexplored avenue that could provide very interesting large-scale applications. The first is in terms of ease of networking.

> *When I was teaching concurrently, at times links for different Google Meets and events were flying around so fast I couldn't keep track of them. As I had children in multiple places at the same time, I had to have a way to seamlessly and regularly deliver links to children in a way that was accessible and easy for them to understand. Using a map of the school, I inserted dots on the map in the real-life location of the meeting. When another teacher was hosting a Google Meet or there was a livestream we needed to attend, I would put the link into the dot of her classroom on the map. In this way, the children were able to hop around quickly and easily from Meet to Meet, event to event.*
>
> *– Heidi*

The application is that a child sitting in a fourth-grade classroom could be virtually attending a math session in another class or meeting with a student in another grade, while their classmate worked on another project or met with a teacher. The children could be physically in the room, but digitally everywhere, all over the map. Applied to working more globally, this networked method is one where schools and programs could be linked together with such an easy method of collaboration and connection, children can operate the system easily and independently.

Finally, it is interesting to think of the slides as large digital classroom panels that begin to form a 3D space. It is interesting to think about the digital classroom as a sort of precluding immersive experience that keeps children safely and firmly planted in the physical world, playing, and working socially, safely and cooperatively with friends and peers to discover and learn digital tools and technologies.

Using digital objects as representational portals to new worlds of educational exploration is an easy and effective way to integrate technology in a balanced, healthy, and accessible way for children. The digital classroom allows children to see themselves in a rich world of digital creativity, discovery and imagination while simultaneously providing learners with opportunities for in-person social experiences, academics, and play.

Resources

While there are many more resources available, these are good places to start developing your own digital classroom.

Math:
Bridges in Mathematics Apps https://www.mathlearningcenter.org/apps
Berkeley Everett https://berkeleyeverett.com/
Mathigon https://mathigon.org/
MathsBot https://mathsbot.com/
University of Cambridge https://nrich.maths.org/9086

Literacy:
Epic https://getepic.com
Padlet https://padlet.com/
Ranger Rick https://rangerrick.org/
StoryboardThat https://storyboardthat.com
Storyline Online https://storylineonline.net
Voki https://voki

General Educational Games and Tools:
PBS Kids https://pbskids.org/
Math Playground https://www.mathplayground.com/
Chaarani, B., Ortigara, J., Yuan, D., Loso, H., Potter, A., & Garavan, H.P. (2022). Association of video gaming with cognitive performance among children. *JAMA Network*, 5(10), e2235721. doi:10.1001/jamanetworkopen.2022.35721

References

Bediou, B., Adams, D.M., Mayer, R.E., Tipton, E., Green, C.S., & Bavelier, D. (2018). Meta-analysis of action video game impact on perceptual, attentional, and cognitive skills. *Psychological Bulletin*, 144(1), 77–110. https://doi.org/10.1037/bul0000130. Epub 2017 Nov 27. Erratum in *Psychological Bulletin*, 144(9), 978–979, 2018. PMID: 29172564.

For Product Safety Concerns and Information please contact our EU
representative GPSR@taylorandfrancis.com
Taylor & Francis Verlag GmbH, Kaufingerstraße 24, 80331 München, Germany

www.ingramcontent.com/pod-product-compliance
Lightning Source LLC
Chambersburg PA
CBHW050633300426
44112CB00012B/1785